CULINARY MAGIC TRICK
Great Grilling and Smoking Made Easy

Adam Fisher

Copyright © 2021 Adam Fisher

All rights reserved.

ISBN: 9798665296562
Fisher Independent Publishing

DEDICATION

This book is dedicated to everybody who loves to cook over fire and smoke…and to the competition Barbecue teams I have had the honor of being a part of:

"Sultans of Swine" Columbia SC
"Tastes Like More" Greenville SC

ACKNOWLEDGMENTS

The author recommends Spears Acres seasonings and sauces to provide the best taste for your grilling and smoking endeavors.

Rusty's All Purpose Rub, Spears Acres Traditional Sweet BBQ Sauce, Rusty's Red Neck Rub, Spears Acres Kickin Sweet Sauce, and others are now available to the public.

Visit **spearsacres.com** to order.

Special Thanks to Rusty Spears, Rob Myers, Caroline Kinsler Wade, Steve Brooks, Mike Clifton, Mac Jenkins, Susan King, Chuck Hill, Chris Cousins, Tim Kersey, Paul Manville, Cal Harrison, Angela Harrison, John Southard, and Mama Fisher for helping me endeavor to learn more about the culinary arts.

CONTENTS

1	Origin of the Name	1
2	Lingo, Parlance, and Jargon	2
3	The Grill	5
4	The Smoker	25
5	Marinades & Sauces	31
6	Grilled Beef and Pork	55
7	Grilled Chicken	71
8	Grilled Vegetables	85
9	Grilled Seafood	103
10	Now for Smoking	115

1 ORIGIN OF THE NAME

It was approaching 6 am when the conductor pulled the train into Ridgeway, SC on a cold November Saturday morning. He had done this every year. The area of track where he came to a standstill was the middle of a large grass field. A field that was lined with some 80 BBQ smokers and their cooking teams.

Behold, the annual *"Pig On The Ridge"* barbecue cookoff championships. The smoke from all 80 cooking machines was wafting through the air with the most pleasant of aromas as he walked over to our setup for a sample of our pulled pork.

The sun was coming up on the horizon as he spoke. His breath produced the likeness of fog in the cold winter air as he proclaimed, "Yall got this thing going on ain't you. It's kind of like a culinary magic trick around here."

And indeed it was.

2 LINGO, PARLANCE, AND JARGON

Barbecue Terminology

Hogma: Term by some BBQ pundits that pork is the only legitimate barbecue meat.

Southern Crutch: Preserving pork butt's post-fire life by wrapping it in foil, then 3 towels, then put in empty ice chest for 1 ½ hours to rest, in order to retain moisture and flavor.

Power Cook: If a pitmaster is behind on cooking and must crank up the heat to overcompensate.

Butt Over Brisket: When pork butt is cooked atop brisket and its juices flow down through the grate to baste the beef.

Shiggin: A covert practice where slick pitmasters spy on competitors to uncover (and steal) BBQ secrets.

Quarter T: Turning steak, burgers, or chicken breast ¼ turn counter clockwise halfway through cooking on each side to create diamond grill marks.

Stabbing: Injecting a syringe of marinade into the meat to infuse extra flavor.

Mop: Basting sauce (usually thin vinegar based) on meat before and during cooking to add flavor and carmelization.

Bark: The flavorful outer layer of crust that forms on a brisket or pork butt.

Money Muscle: A tender, well marbled section of pork butt, located high on the shoulder, which is extremely moist and flavorful. As the name implies, it often pulls in the most prize money and trophies on the competition circuit.

Pit Boss: (aka **The Pitmaster**) The sweaty, greasy, tireless culinary artist who presides over the smoker to create char-encrusted proteins of perfection.

Burnt Ends: Charred, crispy, bark in bite sized pieces of smoked brisket. These delicious morsels are also known as "meat candy".

Mr. Brown: (aka **Bark**) The dark, crunchy exterior of whole-hog barbecue.

Miss White: The light, moist interior of whole-hog barbecue.

Mr. Brown Goes To Town: Adding crunchy pieces of pork bark to sandwiches.

Shiner: When a rack of ribs bares exposed bones due to too much meat having been butchered off. The bones "shine through" the meat, and these cuts of pork should be avoided.

Red Hots: Grilled hot dogs or sausages.

White Sauce: A specialty of northern Alabama that is comprised of mayo and vinegar-based sauce, traditionally used on chicken or pork.

Egghead: A fanatic of using the "Big Green Egg" ceramic smoker.

Bone Bird: Bone-in grilled or smoked chicken.

Cascade: The gush of juice that should come forth when brisket is done right.

Smoke Ring: A ribbon of pink meat found beneath the bark of a brisket, caused by the interaction of nitric oxide and myoglobin, the protein that gives flesh it's red color.

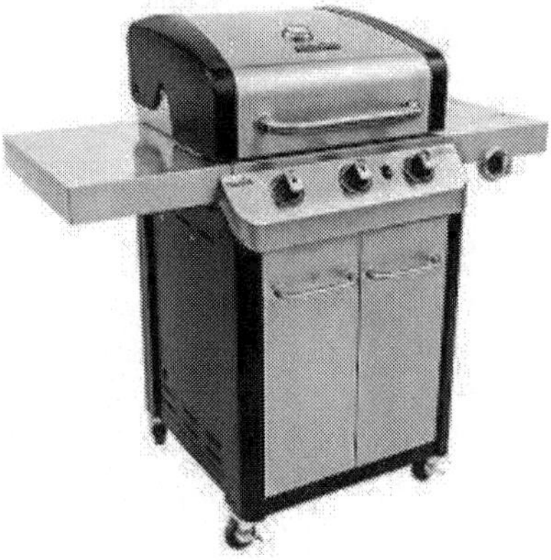

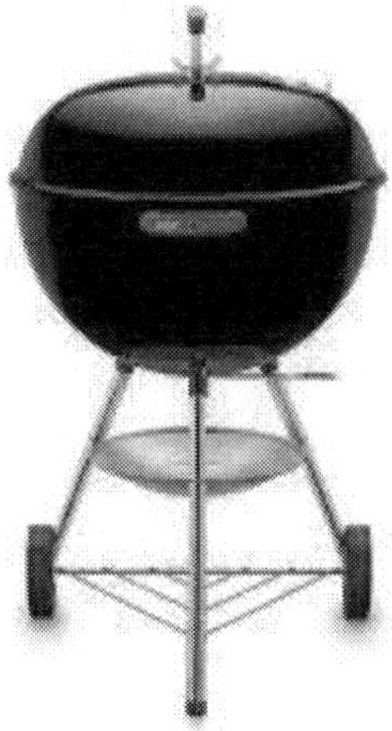

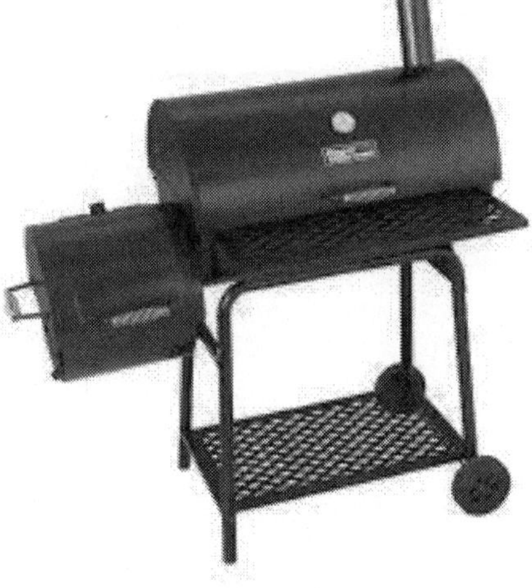

3 THE GRILL

The primary purpose of this book is to provide insight into grilling and smoking meats. These are two totally different cooking methods with totally different finished product. But each can help you make your own culinary magic tricks with relative ease.

To grill is to cook over direct heat, be it fire or charcoal. There are two ways of going about this. One is the charcoal grill. The charcoal method is simply fantastic if done right. But it is also more labor intensive, messy, and time consuming. The other alternative is to use a gas grill. You can fire it up quick & easy and there are no ashes to deal with after the fact. For my average grilling endeavors I use my gas grill because I like convenience.

So let's start with a gas grilling tip. The first recommendation is to keep an **extra full tank of propane** on hand (in the garage, shed, or storage room). When the first tank runs out you can make the switch and reload in a matter of minutes. The last thing you want is to have to run out to the store in the middle of a cook session - and these days it can be hit or miss with them having an available supply. So spare yourself the headache and keep stock on hand.

Preheating the grill is the next step. Just because the fire is hot doesn't mean the grill is ready to cook on. The reality is that fire might be producing plenty of radiant heat - that's the infrared heat you can feel on your hand when you hold it above the grill - but the grill grates themselves are still relatively cool, which means that your food will not receive much conductive heat (the heat transferred directly by the grill grates). Rather than picking up dark, attractive grill marks and releasing easily, your food will stick to the metal. And meat sticking to metal is an actual chemical bond that is nearly impossible to cleanly break. Instead of coming up cleanly, your food tears and shreds. With pre-heated grill grates, your food has much less of a chance of sticking, as proteins alter their shape the minute they come in direct contact with the metal. A good ten minutes at max flame is appropriate.

It's now time to **clean the grill grates**. You may be thinking that it's not necessary: fire kills everything, burnt-on food adds flavor, nobody will notice. Never skip this step. Use a grill brush to clean any char or debris off the grate. Best practice is not to clean the grill at the end of the evening when it has already cooled down and the gunk hardened. Instead clean it after preheating during your next cook.

It is important to purchase a **new grill brush** at least once a year. This is a good investment because it alleviates the chance of worn bristles dislodging and possibly winding up in your food.

No sticking. No poking. When it's time to put the food on, I use a quick shot of Pam no stick cooking spray on both sides of what is to be cooked. This usually helps take care of the problem of food sticking to the grill during cooking and is especially important when dealing with delicate items like seafood or vegetables. Adjust the heat to what the recipe recommends and add the food. Puncturing the meat must be avoided at all costs. Most of the time using metal tongs is the way to go when turning. Never use a cooking fork with steaks or chops because if you pierce the meat, the juices will drip out and leave the meat dry and tough.

Timing is everything. Keep track of your cooking time. Winging it can be costly. And stay nearby so you can react if a flame up problem needs attention. Having a spray bottle filled with water handy will help you remedy this situation.

Get in the zone. Using a two-zone fire can be very helpful in making sure you don't burn the exterior of the meat while the inside is still finishing it's journey to medium rare. With a gas grill this means lighting the burners on one side and leaving the other side off or on very low heat. On a coal grill, this means evenly distributing the coals under only half of the grill, leaving the other half either empty or covered with a very, very thin layer of coals. With two zones you have much more control over your cooking. Place meat and vegetables over the hot side for fast searing, or shift them over to the cooler side for more gently cooking. With your meat on the cool side of the grill and the grill covered, you can even create an oven-like setting inside for grill-roasting large cuts of meat like prime rib or leg of lamb.

No peeking. *If you looking you ain't cooking.* Is it done yet?... Nope. Is it done yet?... Avoid that unbreakable, irresistible urge you get to keep checking on that steak. Repeatedly lifting the lid with a gas grill will cause it to lose heat, making your food sear and cook more slowly. Repeatedly lifting with a coal grill will do the opposite, allowing in oxygen that causes the coals to bun hotter than you'd like them to, resulting in burnt meat. So be patient! It's not a crime to flip your burgers or steaks multiple times as they cook, but just bear in mind that every time you open and close that lid, you're adding inconsistencies to your cooking temperature. Remember this basic rule of thumb: If you're cooking on a gas grill, opening the lid will make it cooler. If you're cooking on a charcoal grill, opening the lid will make it hotter.

Beware the flame. The difference between cooking indoors and cooking outside is that live fire right? So it must be good to let your burgers and steaks get engulfed in flames. But flames engulfing your meat end up leaving sooty, nasty-tasting deposits on the surface of your food. Small flames and minor flare-ups are ok, but you definitely don't want that fire licking your steak before you do.

Culinary Magic Trick

Fire requires three things to burn: fuel, energy, and oxygen. Flare-ups are generally caused by fat dripping out of your meat and igniting on the coals or the grill bars below – essentially adding fuel.

Trimming off excess fat can help mitigate some of the issues, but the fact is that with a well-marbled steak or a nice juicy burger, you *want* that fat to be there from the start. The easiest way to control a flare-up if you aren't cooking too many things at once is to simply move the meat off of the hot side and onto the cool side of the grill until the flare-up subsides before carefully returning it.

But what if your grill is too full to effectively shift things around? This scenario leaves you with two options: reduce the energy in the system or cut off oxygen supply. Squirting water from a spray bottle at little flare ups will do a good job of reducing energy - that energy that was going to feeding the flare-up instead goes into evaporating the water. But it's also a good way to spray up excess soot or worse, to spread around the fat, exacerbating the flare-up problem down the line.

Better is to simply do what you should be doing anyway: close that lid and cut off the oxygen supply. A few moments with the lid *and vents* closed should choke off any flame.

Vent properly. *Grill vents are not there for decoration. They have purpose.* Adjusting the position of the vents is the best way to control oxygen and heat flow within your charcoal grill.

Remember, access to oxygen can have a major impact on how

efficiently your coals combust. Too much and they can erupt into soot-inducing flames. Too little and they choke themselves out.

The lower and upper vents on your charcoal grill can be used to adjust the flow of oxygen, thereby adjusting the heat generated inside your grill. Cooking chicken, ribs, or brisket low and slow over indirect heat? Keep those vents closed. Searing the outside of a big fat steak or a burger? Keep them open to encourage higher heat (just don't let those flames hit the meat!).

The relative positioning of the top and bottom vents can also make a difference. I like to position my vents with the lower vent on the opposite side of the food and the lid vents directly above the food to promote convection currents inside that more efficiently take hot air above and around the food.

Sauce at the end. Don't add the sauce too early. Adding layer after layer doesn't make the food taste better. Barbecue sauce added too soon actually starts to burn and turns acrid way before your meat is even close to completion. Your guests may sheepishly scrape off the layer of blackened soot from what used to be chicken before adding extra sauce straight from the bottle to cover up that bitterness, but it doesn't help. The bitterness stays. All. Night. Long.

Barbecue sauce does very little penetrating no matter how early you apply it. At most it's a surface treatment, which means that you can add it towards the end of cooking and still get just as much flavor out of it without risking burning it. If you are using a sweet barbecue

Culinary Magic Trick

sauce, wait until the final five to 10 minutes of cooking to paint it onto the meat with a brush.

Now for the charcoal method. Don't use lighter fluid or match light charcoal. I once had a friend who used some gasoline to start the charcoal to cook our steaks. We ain't friends no more. If you saturate the coals in liquid fuel, of course they'll light faster! It's logical and it's a mistake most beginners make. It doesn't help that match-light coals and lighter fluid are heavily marketed in the grilling aisle at the home centers and supermarkets. It's easy to understand why so many people buy lighter fluid: Try holding a match underneath a coal and you won't get very far.

After erupting in a mushroom cloud of fire, the flames quickly subside and die. You end up squirting more lighter fluid on the coals in a desperate attempt to keep the fire going (and perhaps even after the fire is alive and kicking because it's just so damn fun to set things on fire). All seems to be going well until you take that first gasoline-scented bite of a hamburger. The truth is this - no matter how long you let a fire that was started with lighter fluid burn, you can taste it on your food, and it's not pleasant.

Use a **Charcoal Chimney.** You place some crumpled newspaper underneath it, pack the top with coals, set the newspaper on fire with a single match or lighter, then let it work its magic as oxygen is drawn up and through the coals, lighting them efficiently without the need for any lighter fluid at all. I recommend putting a piece of aluminum foil under the charcoal chimney so that once the coals are ready you can fold up the newspaper ashes, throw them away, and not have them lingering at the bottom of your cooking coals. And please remember, **never** use a charcoal grill indoors. You run the risk of carbon monoxide poisoning. And that's guaranteed to ruin the evening.

Gray is good. Don't spread the coals until they are fully gray. But I'm hungry now you say! I get it. When you have a spatula in your hand, everything looks like a burger. You just can't wait to get that food on the grill, gray ash be damned. But if you start cooking before your coals are ready, it will lead to inconsistent heat, off-flavors, and unpredictable cook times. In a nutshell, bad results.

Have patience. There's a reason the bag tells you to wait until the coals are covered in gray ash. A fire that might seem moderately hot while the coals still have some black will very rapidly rise to inferno levels as the coals continue to ignite. Temperature control is priority number one when it comes to grilling, and waiting until those coals stabilize is the best way to avoid any surprises.

Keep it simple. Don't cook too many things at once. Some people like chicken, some people like sausages, some people like burgers, why not cook them all at once?

Here's why: Your burgers overcook, your chicken is undercooked, everything is cross-contaminated, and nothing is as good as it should be. Stick to grilling one type of food at a time but focus on really nailing it. The high heat you need for perfectly seared burgers or steaks is different from the low-and-slow heat you need for chicken or sausages. When I'm having a cookout, I'll focus on cooking one type of meat at a time before moving on to the next, making sure that I have plenty of side dishes and snacks for folks who don't like the particular thing I'm cooking at the moment. The result is better food and happier guests…and by default, a happier cook.

Use a thermometer if you need to. Professional chefs on TV poke their steak with their finger to see if it's done. You know the drill: hold your forefinger to your thumb and poke the ball of your thumb with your other hand. That's what rare feels like. Hold your center finger and that's medium. Hold your third finger and that's well-done. In the end, you're liable to get the middle finger from somebody with a burned or raw steak.

Let's face it. You probably are not a professional, which means you probably haven't cooked the hundreds or thousands of steaks required to fine tune your poke-test finger. Your steak ends up well done or grossly undercooked.

So I've put together a chart that provides basic insight to the most common items you will be grilling. Again, keeping that cooking thermometer nearby is going to pay dividends.

Category	Food and Temperatures	Grill Method
BEEF	Ground Beef 160 Steaks 140 (med) / 130 (med rare)	Direct Heat
PORK	Sausages 165 Pork Chops 145	Direct Heat
CHICKEN and TURKEY	Boneless Breast 165 Bone-In Thigh/Leg 165 Whole 165	Direct Heat Indirect Heat
SEAFOOD	Salmon/Thick Cuts 145 Shrimp/Small Items 145	Direct Heat

So forget about the whole poke test. First off, different people have different fingers, different hands, and entirely different sets of calibration. In addition to that, different steaks all feel, well, different. Without tons and tons of experience, there's no way to reliably tell if your steak is done by poking it. You know what is reliable? Your thermometer.

Give it a rest. Don't serve your food too soon. You want to have the food hot for hungry guests, but patience once again is a key ingredient to great results. Cutting into a steak that's too hot not only ends up burning your mouth, but it also causes the meat to unleash a torrent of juices that run all over the cutting board or plate.
Let your meat rest off of the grill for a few minutes before serving it. This will allow the internal juices to redistribute, which in turn reduces the amount of spillage you get after cutting into them. So you like the outside of your meat to be hot and sizzling right when you serve it? No problem: rest your meat as usual, then right before

serving it toss it back over the highest possible heat on your grill for just around 30 seconds per side. You'll end up with perfectly rested, juicy meat and a nice crisp, sizzling crust.

THE RIDDLE OF RESTING EXPLAINED

Patience can be hard to come by if you've got a sizzling ribeye staring at you, but resting is the highest virtue of steak cooking. Resting after grilling allows juices to redistribute and the internal temperature to even out. The meat becomes plumper and juicier. Resting thicker steaks on a wire rack helps air circulate, preserving that exterior crust.

The Importance of Resting Meat
Instructions on how to be a man: Start large fire. Cook large steaks over large fire. Rip steaks from fire with bare hands, bite down, and allow succulent juices to dribble down chin as tongue gets third degree burns.

Instructions on how to be a *smart* man: Start large fire. Cook large steaks over large fire. Rip steaks from fire with bare hands, allow steaks to rest in a warm place undisturbed for 10 minutes. Bite down, and allow succulent juices to dribble down to your taste buds on the way to your stomach.

So the bottom line is I have to wait before I can get down on that perfectly charred ribeye? Unfortunately, yes.

And here's why:

Soon I will show you a picture of a steak that was cooked on a grill to medium rare (an internal temperature of 125°F). The steak was then immediately placed on a cutting board and sliced in half, whereupon a deluge of juices started flooding out and onto the board. The result: Steak that is less than optimally juicy and flavorful. This tragedy can be easily avoided by allowing your steak to rest before slicing.

The center of the steak becomes **supersaturated** *with liquid.* And this happens because as one surface of the meat hits the grill, the juices in that surface are forced away towards the center, increasing the concentration of moisture in the middle of the steak. Once the steak gets flipped over, the same thing happens on the other side. The center of the steak has become supersaturated with liquid - there's more liquid in there than it can hold on to - so when you slice it open, all that extra liquid pours out. By resting the steaks, you allow all that liquid that was forced out of the edges and into the center time to migrate back out to the edges.

Imagine a steak as a big bundle of straws, each straw filled with liquid, and representing the muscle fibers. As the meat cooks, these straws start to change shape, becoming narrower, and putting pressure on the liquid inside. Since the meat cooks from the outside in, the straws are pinched most tightly at their edges, and slightly less tightly in their center. So far so good. Logically, if the edges are pinched more tightly than the center, liquid should get forced towards the middle, right?

Well here's the problem: water is not compressible. In other words, if you have a two-liter bottle filled to the brim with water, it is (nearly) physically impossible to force more water into that bottle without changing the size of that bottle. Same thing holds true with a steak.

Unless we are somehow stretching the centers of the muscle fibers to make them physically wider, there is no way to force more liquid into them. You can easily prove that the muscle fibers are not getting wider by measuring the circumference around the center of a raw steak vs. a cooked one. If liquid were being forced into the center, the circumference should grow. It doesn't - it may appear to bulge, but that is only because the edges shrink, giving the illusion of a wider center.

In fact, the exact opposite is the case. Since the center of a medium-rare steak comes up to 125°F, it too is shrinking, and forcing liquid out. Where does all that liquid go? To the only place it can: out of the end of the straws (or, the surface of the steak). That sizzling noise you hear as a steak cooks? That's the sound of moisture escaping and evaporating.

So why does an un-rested steak expel more juices than a rested one? It all has to do with temperature. We already know that the width of the muscle fibers is directly related to the temperature to which it is cooked, and to a degree, this change in shape is irreversible. A piece of meat that is cooked to 180°F will never be able to hold on to as much liquid as it could in its raw state. But once that meat has cooled slightly, its structure relaxes. The muscle fibers widen up slightly again, and it's this small change in shape that makes all the difference.

After 10 minutes of resting, the edges of the steak have cooled all the way down to around 125°F, allowing them to suck up even more liquid from the center of the steak. What's more, the center of the steak has by this time cooled down to around 120°F, causing it to widen slightly. Cut the meat open at this stage, and the liquid will be so evenly and thinly distributed throughout the steak that surface tension is enough to keep it from spilling out on the plate.
The difference is dramatic. Here's that picture I was telling you about.

But wait a minute...how do we know that those juices really are staying inside the rested steaks? Is it not possible that in the ten minutes that I've allowed it to rest that the liquid hasn't simply evaporated, leaving me with a steak that is equally un-moist?

To prove this is not the case, all you need to do is weigh the steaks before and after cooking. Aside from a minimal amount of weight loss due to rendered fat, the vast majority of weight loss comes from juices that are forced out of the meat.

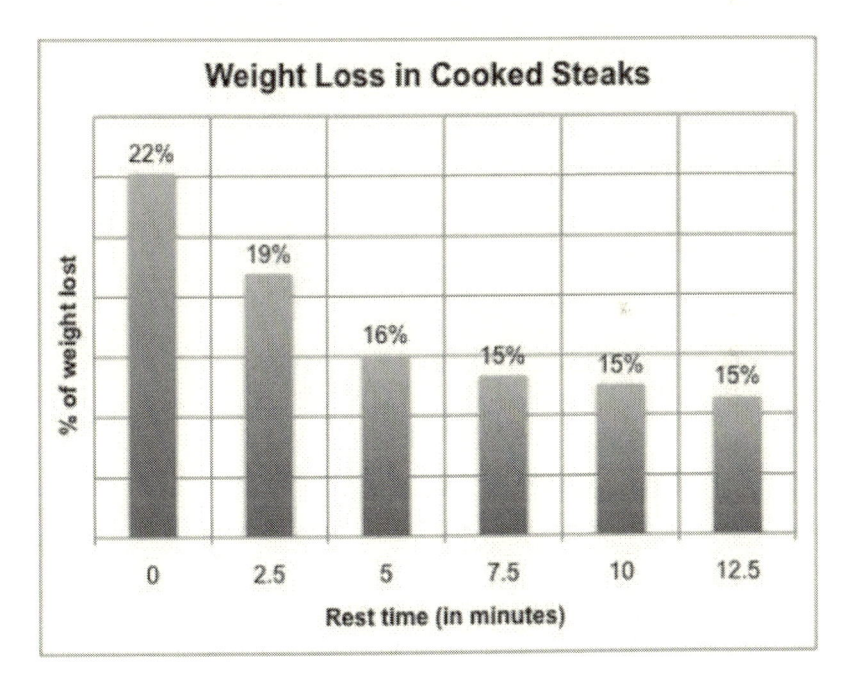

Weight Loss in Cooked Steaks

Rest time (in minutes)	% of weight lost
0	22%
2.5	19%
5	16%
7.5	15%
10	15%
12.5	15%

The steak loses around 13 percent of its weight just during cooking. Cut it open immediately, and you lose an additional nine percent. Combined, that's close to 25% of your steak saying goodbye. But allow it to rest, and you can minimize this additional weight loss down to around an additional two percent.

Larger cuts of meat mean a longer rest.

So we know what's good for steaks, but what about for larger cuts of meat, like a whole roasted pork loin, or a prime rib? Well, the same principles apply here too. But the main difference is they need to rest for longer. How long? Well there are various rules of thumb: five minutes per inch of thickness, ten minutes per pound, half of the total cooking time, etc.

By far the easiest and most foolproof way to test if your meat has rested long enough is the same way you can tell if your meat is cooked properly: with a thermometer.

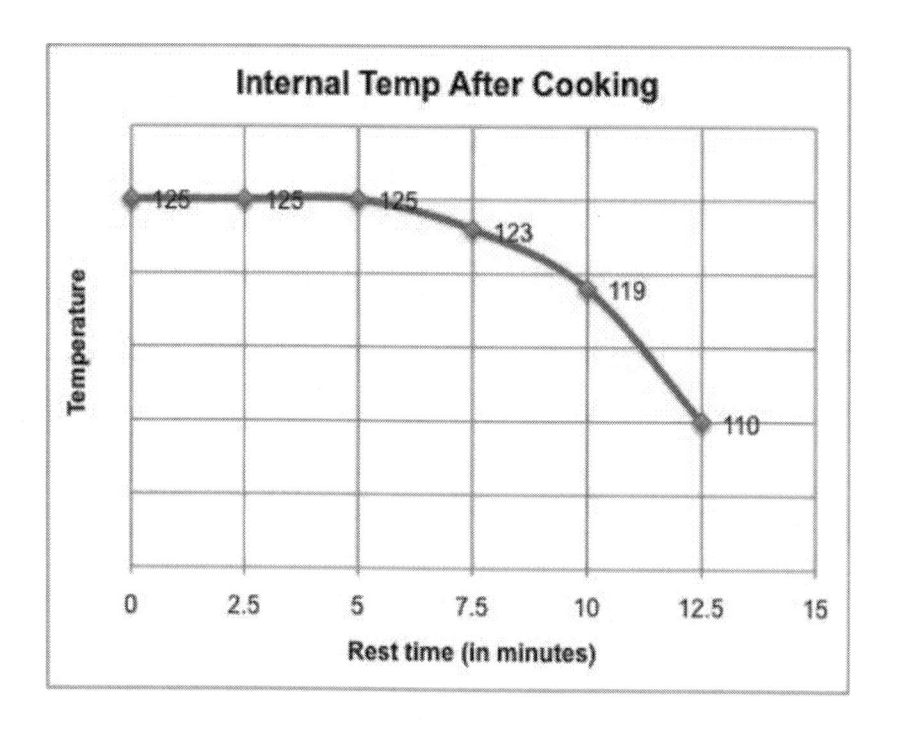

Internal Temp After Cooking

Rest time (minutes)	Temperature
0	125
2.5	125
5	125
7.5	123
10	119
12.5	110

Culinary Magic Trick

Ideally, no matter how well-done you've cooked your meat, you want to allow it to cool down until the very center has reached 120°F. At this stage, the muscle fibers have relaxed enough that you should have no problem with losing juices. As shown in the graph, for a 1.5 inch-thick steak, this translates to around 10 minutes. For a prime rib, this may take as long as 45 minutes.

Enough of the science lesson already! Let's get back to the nitty gritty. Which is performing culinary magic tricks.

Tastes Like More

Details Matter Every Time

Always use **fresh ground pepper**. You can buy a grinder filled with peppercorns for only a few dollars at your local grocery store. This small detail makes a big difference.

Always use **sturdy metal skewers**. Wooden ones burn. Metal skewers also allow food to cook on the inside as well as the outside via transfer of heat. Use skewers that will keep food from rotating. Flat skewers are a favorite. Use high heat. Tender well marbled cuts of steak are best for skewering. Marinade prior to cooking to add flavor and carmelization.

A **grill basket** is the answer to grilling many kinds of vegetables and seafood so your food doesn't fall through the grill grate.

A version of the basket is available for cooking kabobs and is well worth the investment.

Make **diamond grill marks** on all meats. Simply turn the food a quarter turn to the left halfway through cooking on each side.

22

Culinary Magic Trick

Keep meats refrigerated until ready for cooking, then let **sit at room temperature for 15 minutes** before grilling or smoking.

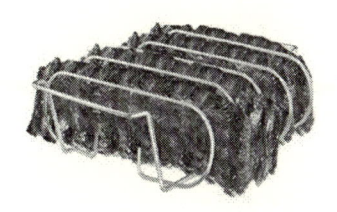

A **"rib rack"** helps maximize your available cooking area both on the grill or in a smoker.

The **Charcoal Chimney** that was discussed earlier can be purchased at your local home improvement store. Always buy quality charcoal. You get what you pay for.

Make sure your cooking knives are **sharp**. Dull knives are dangerous and perform poorly. Don't overlook this small detail. A hand held knife sharpener is a great investment and can also be found at your local stores.

Buy **quality** meat. A trip to your local butcher shop is worth the time and money. Why? The difference is why.
Here in Greenville, SC I go to my neighborhood NY Butcher Shoppe.

Use **fresh** herbs and vegetables when you can. And stock up on quality seasonings so you always have plenty on hand.

ANATOMY OF A CHARCOAL SMOKER

- EXHAUST DAMPER
- TEMPERATURE GAUGE
- LID
- UPPER GRATE
- WATER BOWL
- LOWER GRATE
- SMOKE CHAMBER
- CHARCOAL PAN
- BASE PAN
- INTAKE DAMPERS

4 THE SMOKER

The June afternoon sunshine was the perfect backdrop for an old fashioned "Pig Pickin". I lived only a few minutes from Caughman's Meats, where I knew the staff by name since I frequented it so much. Found out when they would slaughter and showed up shortly thereafter in an old pickup truck. Large sheets of butcher paper were placed in the truck bed as it backed up to the loading dock. Then two kind souls would throw a fresh whole hog onto the paper, causing the truck to dip down a few inches since the average one was 125 pounds dressed out.

From there it was straight to the smoker at my farm. Injected all over with mustard based barbecue sauce and rubbed with spices, it was prepped in no time. For the next 22 hours it would cook at 190 degrees, skin side down. I never flipped it to expose the meat side to the direct heat. Then for two final hours finish the cook at 250 degrees. Open the lid and use a meat cleaver to make random cuts and loosen the tender pork that was emitting steam and smoke. Put a little more mustard BBQ sauce on top and it was ready.

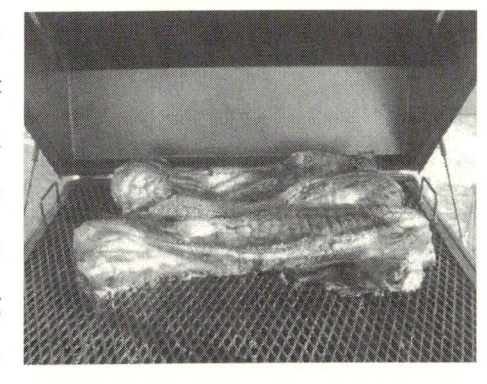

Guests would pull a chunk and grin with delight at the taste. And this would go on for hours. The real treasure was located adjacent to both sides of the spine where for some reason the pork was the absolute best. It was hard not to keep that secret to ourselves. At the end of the day all that was left was the bones of the smoked whole hog. In competitions this method was impossible to replicate because of time constraints. Usually 12 hours or so was all you had from start to finish so adjustments would be made for that. And it was award-winning anyway.

But the smoker can be summed up in two words: **low and slow.** Low heat and slow cooking. And no peeking. "If you lookin you ain't cookin" is the saying, for every time the lid is raised it makes the heat inconsistent. Little details like that matter when preparing a culinary magic trick. Kind of like how Pit Crews in car races keep track of how many pounds of pressure is in each tire…because you are aiming for perfection.

So if you've got the means to do it, smoke a whole hog in the fashion just described and invite a whole bunch of people over to enjoy it. Otherwise, we will be taking a look at alternatives to a 125 pound endeavor. I'm speaking of Pork Butt, Ribs, Chicken, and Brisket. Each of which is a magic trick unto itself.

There are many options when it comes to smokers. My favorite is the **Orion Cooker**. It has never failed me.

Culinary Magic Trick

A basic **"bullet"** smoker is inexpensive and good for the novice cook. The meat cooks in several ways all at once. Heat, steam, and smoke come together to produce the magic. The bottom pan is charcoal and wood chips, above that is the water/drip pan which provides steam, and the two levels above that are for the meat.

The next level of smokers is the **"offset"** model. The charcoal and wood chips are in a separate chamber which spreads the heat and smoke evenly over the meat in the main chamber, ultimately making its way out of the smokestack and into the air to drive your neighbors wild. The ideal temperature is between 225-250 degrees for most cooking. In order to achieve this, charcoal and wood chips will need to be added periodically during the process.

Next we have the smoker that I use most often. It is the **Orion** and you simply put the food in it and light the charcoal. Take the food off at the recommended time and it comes out perfect every time. Charcoal stays on the **outside** around the cook chamber and on top to create convection heat. The wood chips are inside around the perimeter to provide the smoldering smoke. The drip pan is also in the cooking chamber situated below the meats. It provides steam and keeps your items juicy. I have used the Orion for brisket, ribs, turkey, pork butt, chicken, and sausage. It cooks in a fraction of the time compared to a traditional smoker. And it is relatively inexpensive and will last for many years if you take care of it. I've had mine for 10 years already.

The **"Egg"** is a combination kamado (traditional Japanese) grill, ceramic grill & charcoal smoker all in one. It turns out some good results, especially with steak, pork, and ribs. The Egg costs a little more, but can be a wise investment if you will use it regularly.

Finally we get to the whole-hog type smoker. Known as a **super smoker**, it is often a pull behind vehicle model. Among some barbecue fanatics it may be incorporated into an elaborate outdoor kitchen vehicle. Some spend a small fortune on this element of their cooking equipment. The model I use is a standard pull behind with propane heat. This provides a way to keep the temperature consistent at right around 200 degrees. For the smoke, I use a small pan of charcoal on top of the grate where I put wood chips periodically. For the most part it is best to keep the lid closed. If you've got a cook team, and can get a volunteer for the overnight shift, a super smoker with an offset firebox that burns wood or charcoal is a viable option.

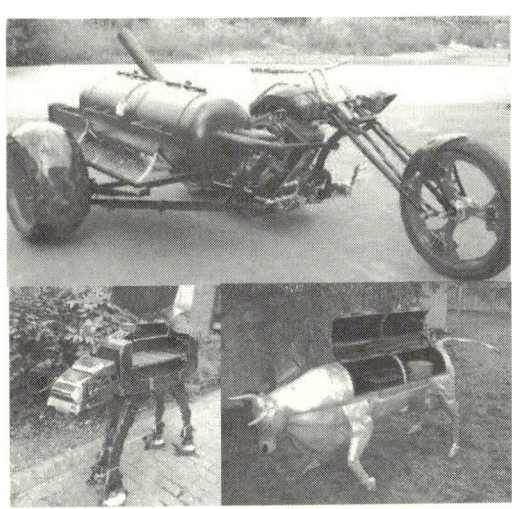

Custom smokers are often creative pieces of art, who's only limitation is one's imagination...and welding equipment.

The final chapter of this book is dedicated to the art of smoking. But we can take a look at some basic tips now:

Boneless Butt (pork shoulder) cooks more evenly so use it when you can for making pulled pork.

Trim off some fat so you can apply rub to more meat surface.

Always **rinse and dry** pork and chicken before prepping with seasoning or marinade.

After laying on rub, **let items sit** overnight, covered, in the fridge.

Cover butts, ribs, brisket **with foil** and let rest 60 minutes after cooking.

After pulling or chopping pork, weed out fat and gristle to throw away, and put the cleaned pork in **crock pot** with sauce for 2 hours on warm before serving.

Infuse flavor by injecting pork butt with Apple Cider Vinegar and adding a coat of mustard.

Get creative and top pork butts with a **layer of bacon**. The smell and taste will be magical.

Purchase a pair of **BBQ Gloves** which can handle high heat.

Keep several **different kinds of wood chips** on hand including Hickory, Cherry, Apple, and Mesquite.

Buy **quality charcoal**. Kingsford is tried and true. Avoid match light charcoal for grilling.

Lining the drip pan with **foil** can make for easier clean up.

5 MARINADES AND SAUCES

What, Why, and How Long	32
Tasty Morsels Marinade	34
Teriyaki Marinade	35
Lemon & Rosemary Marinade	36
Classic Steak Marinade *and variations*	37
Pineapple Marinade	40
Jamaican Jerk Marinade	41
Greek Style Marinade	43
Brisket Marinade	45
Mexican Marinade	46
Beef Rib Marinade	48
Korean Sesame Marinade	50
Mustard BBQ Sauce	52
Crowin' Gamecock BBQ Sauce	53
Herbed Lemon Butter Sauce	54

What Does a Marinade Do? The primary purpose of a marinade is to infuse meat, fish, or vegetables with flavor. A side benefit is that the acid in a marinade (usually vinegar, lemon juice, or wine) helps to break down the tough connective tissue of some cuts of meat to make it tender.

Because marinades contain an acid, marinating should always be done in a glass, ceramic, stainless steel, or plastic container - never in aluminum because it will react with this metal and render an off taste to the food.

Marinating times depend on the type of food.

Marinate beef, lamb, and pork for about six to 12 hours. It can remain in the marinade for up to five days.

Marinate poultry for up to four hours. It can remain in the marinade safely for up to two days.

Marinate fish or vegetables for 30 minutes to one hour.

Marinate shrimp for 15 to 30 minutes. Do not marinate longer or they will get mushy.

Marinade Safety

The marinade will be contaminated by bacteria from the meat, poultry, fish, or seafood and it isn't strong enough to kill the bacteria.

You must always keep food refrigerated while it is marinating. If you will be grilling away from home, keep it well-iced in a cooler.

It is safest to discard the marinade once it has been in contact with the raw food. Don't use the marinade to baste meats or vegetables on the grill or use it as-is for a sauce. Keep the contaminated marinade away from items you will serve uncooked.

It is not recommended, but you can make the used marinade safe by placing it in a saucepan and bringing it to a boil. Reduce the heat to medium-low and simmer for 6 to 8 minutes. You can use it over sliced meats or add it to rice.

Popular Marinades for Meat or Vegetables

Marinades are probably the most important ingredient to any cookout. A good marinade not only keeps your grilling moist and flavorful, but makes it healthier.

Marinating is best done in a sealed environment. Using a zip lock bag and squeezing as much of the air out as possible is recommended. I also put the bag in a pan in the refrigerator just in case there is a leak. Experience has taught me that cleaning up marinade drippings in your refrigerator is a drag.

These marinades are some of my favorite. They all will work with most everything.

Tasty Morsels Marinade

Use this versatile marinade to lend zesty flavor to chicken, beef, pork, or vegetables.

Ingredients:
- 3/4 cup olive oil
- 1/2 cup soy sauce
- 1/4 cup Worcestershire sauce
- 1/4 cup balsamic vinegar
- 2 tablespoons lemon juice
- 2 tablespoons Dijon mustard
- 1 teaspoon fresh ground pepper
- 3 cloves garlic, finely chopped
- 1 tablespoon finely chopped fresh parsley

Whisk all ingredients together in a bowl. Pour marinade over chicken, steak, pork, or vegetables. Cover and chill for at least 5 hours. Using a zip lock bag makes clean up easy. Remove meat from marinade, discarding marinade. Pat items dry and cook as desired.

Tip: Try this one with beef and vegetable kabobs.

Teriyaki Marinade

Want to get that great teriyaki flavor into your favorite dish? This marinade is sure to add flavor to whatever you're grilling. This marinade works particularly well with pork and poultry. You can make an extra batch, simmer it until thickened and drizzle on top of sliced grilled meats and vegetables.

Ingredients:
- 1 cup soy sauce
- 1/2 cup water
- 3/4 cup brown sugar (packed)
- 1 tablespoon distilled white vinegar
- 1 tablespoons vegetable oil
- 3 medium green onions (both white and green parts, finely sliced)
- 4 cloves garlic (minced)

Combine all ingredients in a medium bowl. Stir gently until sugar is completely dissolved. Use immediately or store in a refrigerator, covered for 6 to 7 days after preparation.

Marinading Times (approximate)

Beef, pork, and lamb for 4 to 24 hours.
Chicken and other poultry for 2 to 12 hours.
Fish, seafood, vegetables, and meat substitutes for 1 hour.

Tips: If using as a sauce, bring ingredients to a medium simmer. Stir occasionally and watch for burning. Reduce heat as needed. Let mixture simmer for 5 to 6 minutes. If still runny, then thicken with cornstarch as follows:

Dissolve 2 teaspoons cornstarch in 2 tablespoons water. Turn heat up to medium-high and add mixture, stir in for 30 seconds to activate the cornstarch. Remove from heat, let mixture thoroughly cool, and use.

Try this one with chicken and vegetable kabobs.

Lemon and Rosemary Marinade

Looking for a way to brighten up the flavor of your chicken dish? This lemon and rosemary marinade is a great solution. Not only does it work really well with chicken, but it tastes excellent with pork too.

Just add the ingredients to a medium-sized plastic bag or glass bowl, add your protein of choice, and then let marinate for about 1 to 2 hours.

If you are doing meal prep, you can make this mixture ahead of time and store it in an airtight container in the refrigerator for up to a week, or in the freezer for up to 3 months.

Ingredients:

- 3 large lemons
- 1/4 cup fresh rosemary (or 2 tablespoons dried rosemary)
- 1/4 cup olive oil
- 1 to 2 cloves garlic (minced)
- 2 teaspoons salt
- 1/2 teaspoon white pepper

Cut lemons in half and squeeze out the juice into a medium plastic or glass bowl. Add remaining ingredients and mix well.

Marinate chicken or pork for 1 to 2 hours in the mixture. The mixture can be made ahead of time and stored in an airtight container in the refrigerator for 1 week and in the freezer for up to 3 months.

Tip: Try this one with bone-in chicken legs and thighs.

Classic Steak Marinade

A high-quality steak doesn't need any help. A not-so-great steak, on the other hand, can definitely benefit from a good marinade.
If you are grilling a steak, particularly leaner cuts like flat-iron, skirt, flank steak, and London broil, then it is wise to marinate them first.

This steak marinade recipe is considered a wet marinade (versus a dry rub) and provides just enough acid to help tenderize 1 1/2 pounds of steak but also infuses the outer layer with delicious flavor. If you will be grilling more than 1 1/2 pounds of meat, simply double, triple, or quadruple the marinade ingredients.

Ingredients:
- 1/4 cup red wine vinegar
- 2 tablespoons Worcestershire sauce
- 1/4 cup olive oil (or avocado oil)
- 1 1/2 teaspoons sea salt
- 2 teaspoons fresh oregano (finely chopped)
- 1/2 teaspoon fresh ground pepper
- 1/2 teaspoon fresh thyme (finely chopped)
- 1/4 teaspoon onion powder (or granulated onion)
- 1 to 2 cloves garlic (minced)

Place red-wine vinegar and Worcestershire sauce in a bowl and whisk together. Slowly drizzle in olive oil or avocado oil, whisking constantly, until well combined.

Add sea salt, oregano, pepper, thyme, onion powder, and minced garlic, and stir until well combined. Let the mixture stand at room temperature for 5 minutes or so before using.

Place steak in a resealable plastic bag and pour the marinade over the top, massaging it into the meat and making sure all surfaces are coated well.

Seal the bag, put it on a rimmed pan to catch any escaping juices or in a shallow bowl and place in the refrigerator for about 2 1/2 hours. Marinating time for beef depends on the cut and thickness.

Once the meat is marinated, it's time to grill according to your preferred method. This marinade can be made ahead of time and stored in an airtight container in the refrigerator for up to five days.

Recipe Variations
Balsamic vinegar can be used in place of the red wine vinegar, and teriyaki sauce instead of Worcestershire sauce.

Lemon, orange, or lime zest can be added for brightness, and whole black, red, or pink peppercorns can be used in place of ground black pepper.

The herbs can be adjusted according to your palate. For a Mexican flavor, try using adobo instead of Worcestershire, cilantro in place of fresh thyme, and adding a few sliced jalapeños.

A great steak doesn't need any help. A not so great steak does. If you are grilling a steak that isn't the most tender then this classic steak marinade is perfect. While perfect for beef, this marinade also works well with pork, poultry, and lamb.

Tip: Treat yourself to a ribeye or NY Strip with this one.

Pineapple Marinade

This sweet, fruity marinade has the power of pineapple and cider vinegar to work its way into the meat. Add to this a collection of flavors that turn any cut of pork or chicken into something truly great.

Ingredients:

    1 cup crushed pineapple

    1/3 cup soy sauce

    1/3 cup honey

    1/4 cup cider vinegar

    1 to 2 cloves garlic, minced

    1 teaspoon ginger powder

    1/2 teaspoon powdered cloves

Mix all ingredients together in a non-corrosive (non-metal) bowl. Let the mixture sit for 15 minutes before using or store in a glass or plastic airtight container in the refrigerator for up to 7 days.

Tips: The marinade can be stored in the refrigerator for up to 7 days in a glass or plastic airtight container.

To use: Add pork into the mixture for 2 to 8 hours. For chicken, marinate for 2 to 4 hours. The mixture can also be used on vegetables, tofu, fish and seafood with a 15 to 30 minute marinating time.

This marinade works really well on pork or chicken. It is also great for bringing a Hawaiian flavor to beef dishes. The power of pineapple tenderizes and sweetens meats. This is a great pineapple marinade when you don't have a lot of time.

Try this one with thick-cut pork chops.

Jamaican Jerk Marinade

You've heard of Jamaican jerk seasonings and rubs, but this jerk marinade gets that great flavor deep into the meat. Use this mixture on beef, seafood, or poultry - it's also great on most vegetables.

For chicken, the suggested marinating time is two to four hours. Marinate your pork a little longer, about two to eight hours. Vegetables and meat substitutes just need a short dip of roughly 30 to 40 minutes, and if using on fish and seafood, marinate no more than 30 minutes.

Ingredients:
- 1 medium onion (finely chopped)
- 1/2 cup scallions (finely chopped)
- 1 hot pepper (finely chopped)

3 tablespoons soy sauce

1 tablespoon oil

1 tablespoon cider vinegar (or white vinegar)

2 teaspoons fresh thyme leaves

2 teaspoons sugar

1 teaspoon salt (kosher or sea salt is preferable)

1 teaspoon Jamaican Pimento (or ground allspice)

1 teaspoon fresh ground pepper

1/2 teaspoon ground nutmeg

1/2 teaspoon ground cinnamon

Optional: 1 dash hot sauce

Combine all ingredients in a blender and blend until smooth. Depending on size of the blender, this process might need to be done in batches.

Use marinade right away or, if making ahead, simply store in an airtight container and keep in the refrigerator for up to 7 days. I recommend making this the day before using to let the flavors combine well; however, it is not required.

Tip: Try this marinade with bone-in chicken wings.

Greek-style Marinade

This Greek-style marinade can be applied to any meat but works particularly well on lamb and chicken. Let the meat marinate for several hours so the flavors can get infused. You can double or triple this recipe if you are using it on a leg of lamb or a larger quantity of meat.

When you marinate meat, you are soaking it in a seasoned, often acid-based liquid before you cook it. This process imparts flavor to the meat while it is immersed in the liquid. In addition to adding flavor, this process will often tenderize tougher cuts of meat. The soaking process can take minutes or days depending on the type of meat, the type of cut, the amount, and the marinade used.

When you tenderize a cut of meat, what is actually happening is the acid in the marinade is causing the tissue to break down, allowing more moisture to be absorbed by the meat, resulting in a preparation that is juicier.

It is important to balance your marinade. Too much acid can be detrimental to the meat, stripping the outer layer, and failing to penetrate the rest of the cut. A good marinade has a balance of acid, oil, and spice.

Ingredients:

    2 lemons (juiced)

    1/4 cup olive oil

    2 to 3 cloves garlic (minced)

    2 tablespoons fresh oregano leaves (finely chopped)

    1 teaspoon fresh thyme (roughly chopped)

    1 whole bay leaf

    1 teaspoon sea salt

    1/4 teaspoon fresh ground pepper

Juice two lemons into a small bowl. Slowly drizzle olive oil into the lemon juice while whisking. This will help to emulsify the mixture. Add the remaining ingredients and stir. Allow the mixture to stand at room temperature for 10 minutes before using.

Tips: You can use this marinade on all cuts of lamb. Plan on marinating chops and small cuts for about 4 to 5 hours. Large cuts (double recipe) like leg of lamb should be marinated for 8 to 24 hours. Double or triple the recipe for larger cuts.
Store mixture in an airtight container in the refrigerator for up to 1 week after preparation.

The climate and terrain of Greece have tended to favor the breeding of goats and sheep over cattle, and thus beef dishes are uncommon in traditional Greek cooking. Fish dishes are quite common in coastal regions and on the islands.

Classic Greek-style side dishes that go well with marinated roast leg of lamb include oven-roasted potatoes, orzo pasta, or a crisp Greek salad. Or, you can make Greek-style marinated lamb kebabs with a healthy helping of tzatziki yogurt sauce on the side. The main ingredients that complement most Greek dishes include lemon, olive oil, feta cheese, and fresh herbs.

This Greek-style lamb marinade can be applied to any meat but is particularly good on lamb dishes. Let the meat marinate for a while so the flavors can infuse.

Tip: If you like leg of lamb, you've got to try this one.

Brisket Marinade

Whether you are smoking or grilling a brisket, this marinade will add a lot of flavor and help tenderize the meat.

Ingredients:

    1 1/2 cups red wine

    1/2 cup olive oil

    1 1/2 tablespoons mustard

    1 1/2 tablespoons lemon juice

    1 tablespoon wine vinegar

    1 tablespoon horseradish

    1 1/2 teaspoons salt

    1 teaspoon cayenne pepper (use less or omit if preferred)

1 teaspoon onion powder

1 teaspoon garlic powder

Mix all ingredients together in a small bowl. Pour over brisket and let marinate overnight in the refrigerator, turning occasionally. Remove brisket from marinade and boil remaining marinade for 5 minutes to use as a mop.

Tip: Mixture will keep up to 1 week in refrigerator.

Mexican Marinade

When you are preparing a Mexican-style dish, this marinade can be used for any type of meat, poultry, fish, or seafood. The lime and cilantro flavor blend well together and is not too overpowering.

While it has some spice, you can adjust the heat level by using more or less of the ancho chile powder. While many people love cilantro, it has its detractors, as well. Check with your guests about whether to include it or not.

Marinades such as this one tenderize and enhance flavor. An acid is used (in this case, white vinegar, and lime juice) to help break down tougher tissues. But left for too long, the meat or seafood can become overly tenderized and end up mushy. As well, this tenderizing action allows the tissues to bring in more fluid, so it won't dry out as rapidly when grilled. The salt, spices, and herbs add flavor. You should marinate in a container made of glass or food-grade plastic (including sealable plastic bags). Don't marinate in a metal container as the acid can act on it and it can result in off-flavors as well as possibly etching the container.

Ingredients:
- 1/3 cup white vinegar
- 1/3 cup vegetable oil
- 1/3 cup cilantro (fresh, chopped)
- 1/4 cup water
- 3 cloves garlic (minced)
- Juice of 1 lime
- 1 tablespoon cumin
- 1 tablespoon Mexican oregano (dried)
- 1 tablespoon sea salt
- 2 teaspoons chili powder (mild)
- 2 teaspoons fresh ground pepper
- 1 teaspoon ancho chili powder

Combine all of the marinade ingredients. Store the marinade in a plastic or glass container with a lid. It will keep in the refrigerator for up to five days after preparation.

Tip: Try this one for beef fajitas.

Beef Rib Marinade

This marinade adds a lot of flavor to your beef ribs. The acid from the lemon juice and vinegar will keep beef ribs nice and tender as they grill or smoke. Marinating also allows the meat to hold more liquid so your ribs won't dry out.

While perfect for ribs, this mixture can also be used on flat steaks like skirt steak, flat-iron, hanger, and flank steak. The marinating time for steaks would be 4 to 6 hours.

Cayenne pepper is optional in this recipe. Use it if you prefer spicier ribs or you can leave it out.

Ingredients:

    1/4 cup lemon juice

    1/4 cup white vinegar

    1/4 cup olive oil

    3 tablespoons honey

    4 cloves garlic (crushed)

    1 tablespoon sea salt

    1 teaspoon fresh ground pepper

    Optional: 1 teaspoon cayenne

Mix together all of the ingredients in a small bowl. Place the ribs in a container large enough to lay one rack flat. Pour the marinade over ribs, coating them completely. Make sure to turn the rack of ribs a couple of times so it is coated with the marinade on all sides. Cover the container with plastic wrap and let it sit in refrigerator for 12 to 24 hours. Prepare the smoker. Remove the ribs from the marinade and place them in the smoker.

While the ribs are cooking, you can turn any remaining marinade into a baste for ribs. It's safest to use a portion that wasn't used to marinate the ribs. But if you boil the marinade used on the ribs, it can be used as a basting sauce. Place the marinade into a saucepan and bring it to a rolling boil over medium-high heat for 3 to 4 minutes. Remove and let cool for 5 minutes. Use as a baste for ribs. If you are making marinade ahead of time, store it in an airtight container in the refrigerator for up to 5 days after preparation.

Tips: The container you use for marinating should not be made of metal, as the acids in the marinade can react with metal. Use a plastic or glass container or a large ziplock bag. Discard the bag after using it and do not reuse it.

Be sure to keep your ribs in the refrigerator while they are marinating. Do not leave them out at room temperature or outdoor temperatures. If you are taking them to a cookout, be sure to keep them in an ice chest until you are ready to cook.

If you get too busy to cook the ribs, they can be stored in the marinade in the refrigerator for up to five days.

Korean Sesame Marinade

This is the traditional marinade recipe for Korean "Bulgogi" sesame beef, which is a marinated steak cut into strips and served up on lettuce leaves or rice. This is also a great marinade for any cut of beef.

It can be served with a spicy dipping sauce. This is a really easy dish to make for anyone who is beginning to explore Korean cuisine. Bulgogi is a very versatile dish as it can be the star of your meal or just a simple and tasty appetizer.

Ingredients:
- 1/2 cup soy sauce
- 1/3 cup sugar
- 3 tablespoons sake (or rice wine or sherry)
- 2 tablespoons sesame oil
- 8 cloves garlic (minced)
- 4 scallions (minced)
- 2 tablespoons toasted sesame seeds
- 1/2 teaspoon fresh ground pepper

Heat sesame oil in a small saucepan. Add garlic and cook for one minute. Add remaining ingredients, except green onions, and let the sauce cook over medium heat for 3 to 4 minutes, or until the sugar has dissolved completely. Add green onions, promptly remove from heat and let the mix cool completely before using as a marinade.

Tip: To toast sesame seeds place them in a hot saute pan and gently toss until they start to brown. This takes just a few seconds. Pour off into a bowl.

Try this one with thin sliced flank steak.

I use Spears Acres Traditional Sweet BBQ Sauce and Kickin Sweet Sauce on a regular basis for much of my grilled and smoked items.

Here are some others for you to make at home:

(Keep in Mason Jars refrigerated)

BBQ Mustard Sauce

Perfect for Smoked Chicken or Pork

1 quart prepared mustard
1 Tbsp. dry mustard
1 Tbsp. salt
1 Tbsp. fresh ground pepper
½ tsp. red pepper flakes ground
1 cup apple cider vinegar
1 cup water
8 tb margarine or butter (one stick)

Melt butter in saucepan. Add other ingredients and mix well. Simmer 10 minutes, stirring occasionally. Keeps well in refrigerator.

Tip: This is excellent on pulled pork.

Crowin' Gamecock Vinegar Based BBQ Sauce

Great for Boston Butt or Whole Hog

60 oz Apple Cider Vinegar

2 cups Dark Brown Sugar

4 Tbsps. Salt

1 ½ Tbsps. Chili Powder

1 ½ Tbsps. Fresh Ground Pepper

1 Tbsp Cayenne Pepper

1 ½ Tbsps. Onion Powder

1 ½ Tbsps. Garlic Powder

½ Tbsp. White Pepper

Shake Well. Best if allowed to sit in refrigerator for at least 2 weeks, shaking periodically.

*This makes a large batch so you can give some away to friends. Cut ingredients in half if you don't have any friends.

Tip: Offer several different sauces for your guests to try on their pork or chicken.

Herbed Lemon Butter

Great for topping a steak or chicken breast

½ stick butter softened
1 Tbsp. chopped fresh parsley
1 Tbsp. fresh lemon juice
½ tsp. granulated garlic

Mix butter, parsley, lemon juice, and garlic. Place mixture in plastic wrap, roll into log shape, and refrigerate until firm.

Tip: Melt in microwave and serve in small bowls for seafood dishes.

6 GRILLED BEEF AND PORK

Techniques	56
Easy Street London Broil	58
Key West Flank Steak	59
No Jabroni Steak	60
Prime Time Pork Chops	61
Spice Crusted Steak *with Herb Lemon Butter*	62
Teriyaki Ribeye *Pittsburgh Style*	63
Sweet Mustard Pork Loin	64
Garlic Herb London Broil *with Chimichurri Sauce*	65
Showstopper Burgers	66
Beef and Veggie Skewers	68
Texas Twinkies	69

A basic great steak starts with quality meat. A trip to your local butcher is worth the time and money. If possible, spend a little more and buy the PRIME cuts. Salt and pepper each side and apply light coating of non-stick spray (Pam). Grill at the maximum temperature your grill allows. Monitor time and meat temps. A cooking thermometer is a good investment and will pay dividends.

Techniques

Slashing: Increase the surface area for more flavor. This works especially well for less expensive cuts of meat such as London Broil, Flank Steak, or Pork Loin. And it is a technique to be used when smoking Pork Butt. The process calls for adding deep cuts on both sides of the meat before marinating and grilling for more surface area and more of the charred, crispy tips that provide flavor that is out of this world. Cut no more than 1/3 way through and space cuts out to every ¼ inch. Cut cross ways on the other side (if you could see through the steak it would make a diamond pattern). Be sure to use a sharp knife for this technique.

Gville Style: After salt and pepper, add a light coating of sugar to each side and cook at maximum heat to sear. The sugar helps produce a tasty crust on the exterior of the meat. Finish the cook over medium heat for desired doneness.

Carmelization: A deep brown carmelized exterior is the signature of a great steak at some of the world's finest restaurants. You can accomplish a method of this too by

Culinary Magic Trick

adding a glaze to an already seared steak as it finishes cooking. Flip and brush layer after layer. A crusty bark will ensue, akin to the one by Barbecue afficionados.

Here are some popular glazes you may want to try:
Hot sauce (Tobasco, Texas Pete) adds acidity and chile heat.
Blasamic Vinegar lends tartness and a fruity complexity.
Extra Virgin Olive Oil helps carry the rest of the flavors.
Dijon Mustard acts as an emulsifier and nose-clearing spice.
Honey delivers sweetness better than standard white sugar.
Ketchup can back up all the other components.

When I was a kid, we had a family member who would order Filet Mignon Well-Done at the restaurant. This was met with a look of disdain by the waiter and I now know why. So never do that, medium rare is the way to go.

STEAK GRILLING CHART

Thickness	Doneness	Total Minutes
¾"	Rare	6
	Medium	8
	Well	12
1"	Rare	8
	Medium	10
	Well	14
1 ¼"	Rare	9
	Medium	12
	Well	15
1 ½"	Rare	10
	Medium	13
	Well	16

EASY STREET LONDON BROIL

This simple recipe provides great results. It's also a very economical way of serving a grilled beef dish to a large group of guests.

London Broil is a very flavorful piece of beef that can be tough if not marinated, cooked, and sliced properly.

Process is as follows:

1/3 bottle of Italian dressing for marinade
1 2-3 lb. London Broil or Flank Steak (Flank is pricier)

Put meat and marinade in zip lock bag. Then put the bag in a pan to insure no mess.

Refrigerate 12-24 hours, turning once halfway through.

Remove beef from bag and discard marinade. Let sit at room temperature for 15 minutes. Add Salt, Fresh Ground Pepper, and a light coat of Sugar to each side. This will help caramelize the exterior, searing juices in, and creating a crispy crust with a tender middle.

Cook until desired doneness. It is ok to cut into the center while cooking to make sure steak is done to your liking.

Let rest 10 minutes.

Carve across the grain in thin slices. The thinner the better.

Serve slices fanned out and layered on a large platter.

KEY WEST FLANK STEAK

A taste of the Caribbean is on the way. This is another crowd pleaser.

Process is as follows:

1 large red onion, sliced
1 cup minced fresh cilantro
1/4 cup white wine vinegar
1/4 cup Key lime juice
3 tablespoons extra virgin olive oil, divided
6 Key limes, halved
1 beef flank steak (1 ½-2 pounds)
1 teaspoon kosher salt
1/8 teaspoon fresh ground pepper

In a small bowl, combine onion, cilantro, vinegar, lime juice and 2 tablespoons oil until blended. Pour 1 cup marinade into a large bowl or shallow dish. Add lime halves. Rub steak with remaining oil, sprinkle with salt and pepper. Add to bowl; turn to coat. Refrigerate 8 hours or overnight. Cover and refrigerate remaining marinade.

Drain steak, discarding marinade and limes in bowl. Place reserved marinade in a food processor and process until chopped.

Grill steak, covered, over medium heat or broil 4 in. from heat until meat reaches desired doneness (for medium-rare, a thermometer should read 130°; medium, 140°), 6-8 minutes per side. Baste occasionally with reserved marinade. Let stand 10 minutes before thinly slicing steak across the grain.

NO JABRONI STEAK MARINADE

This marinade works great with Rib Eyes or NY Strips, but can be used on any cut of steak.

1/3 cup soy sauce
1/2 cup olive oil
1/3 cup fresh lemon juice
¼ cup Worcestershire sauce
½ tsp. fresh ground pepper
1 ½ tbsps. Garlic powder
3 tbsps. Dried basil
1 ½ tbsps. Dried parsley flakes

Process is as follows:

Mix marinade ingredients well. Put meat and marinade in zip lock bag. Then put the bag in a pan to insure no mess. Refrigerate at least 8 hours, turning once halfway through.

Remove beef from bag and discard marinade. Let sit at room temperature for 15 minutes.

Cook until desired doneness. Let rest 10 minutes.

PRIME TIME PORK CHOPS

This bold marinade adds just the right flavor to grilled pork chops. Use at least 1" thick chops.

Process is a follows:

1 large onion, chopped
2/3 cup butter, melted
1/3 cup cider vinegar
4 teaspoons sugar
1 tablespoon chili powder
2 teaspoons salt
2 teaspoons Worcestershire sauce
1-1/2 teaspoons fresh ground pepper
1-1/2 teaspoons ground mustard
2 garlic cloves, minced
1/2 teaspoon hot pepper sauce

In a small bowl, mix all ingredients. Put chops and marinade in zip lock bag. Then put the bag in a pan to insure no mess.

Refrigerate at least 4 hours, turning once halfway through.

Remove chops from bag and discard marinade. Let sit at room temperature for 15 minutes.

It is recommended that you use a two zone heat to grill. Hot for searing and making the diamond grill marks. Then finishing on the cool side (top closed) for a baking effect.

Let rest 10 minutes before serving.

GRILLED SPICE CRUSTED STEAK WITH HERB LEMON BUTTER

This one requires a little more effort, but the results are worth it. Use at least 1" thick sirloins or a 2-3 lb. flank steak.

Process is as follows:

Herb Lemon Butter
½ stick butter, softened
1 Tbs chopped fresh parsley
1 Tbs fresh lemon juice
¼ tsp granulated garlic

Mix butter, parsley, lemon juice, and garlic. Place mixture in plastic wrap, roll into log shape, and refrigerate until firm.

¼ cup fresh ground black pepper
1 ½ tsp ground white pepper
½ tsp red pepper flakes
1 tsp ground coriander
¼ cup sugar
1 Tbs salt
1 tsp granulated garlic

Combine all spices, mix, and rub spice mixture onto both sides of each steak. Shake off excess. Place on hot grill and cook 4 minutes, turning halfway through. Transfer to cooler section of grill and cook until desired doneness. Let rest 10 minutes.

Serve each steak with a slice of the lemon butter on top.

TERIYAKI RIBEYE PITTSBURGH STYLE

Medium rare on the inside with a crispy light curst on the exterior. Use at least 1 inch thick steaks.

1 cup teriyaki sauce/marinade (store bought)
½ cup extra virgin olive oil
4 10-16 oz. Ribeye Steaks
1 teaspoon fresh ground pepper
1 1/2 tablespoons granulated sugar (regular)

Process is as follows:

Put meat and marinade in zip lock bag.
Refrigerate 12-24 hours, turning once.
Remove steaks, discard marinade. Bring steaks to room temperature (20 minutes on plate).
Preheat Grill to maximum heat.

Spray each steak with pam no stick spray on each side.
Mix pepper and sugar, coat each steak on both sides.

Cook over max high heat 4 minutes, rotate ¼ turn halfway through. Repeat for other side.

Cook until desired doneness (8 minutes total for medium rare).

Let rest 10 minutes before serving.

SWEET MUSTARD PORK LOIN

Classic flavors combine for an excellent main dish.

1/2 cup mayonnaise
1/3 cup red wine vinegar
1/4 cup packed brown sugar
1/4 cup prepared mustard
2 teaspoons seasoned salt
1   3-4 pound pork loin

Process is as follows:

In a small bowl, whisk all ingredients until blended. Put in large ziplock bag with pork loin.

Marinate 4-8 hours in refrigerator. Remove meat and discard marinade. Let stand at room temperature on plate for 20 minutes.

Grill over high heat for 4 minutes per side, rotating ¼ turn halfway through on each side.

Reduce heat to low and move pork from direct heat and cook covered 30 minutes or until desired doneness. Internal temp needs to read at least 165 degrees.

Let rest 10 minutes before slicing and serving.

GARLIC HERB MARINATED LONDON BROIL WITH CHIMICHURRI SAUCE

Medium rare on the inside with a crispy light curst on the exterior. Use at least 1 inch thick steaks.

1/2 Cup Olive Oil
½ Cup Red Wine Vinegar
1 Tbsp. Chopped Fresh Rosemary
½ tsp. dried thyme
4 Cloves garlic, minced
2 shallots, minced
1 Tbsp. fresh ground pepper
1   3 lb. flank steak or London broil

<u>Chimichurri Sauce:</u>
½ Cup Olive Oil
¼ Cup White Wine Vinegar
1 Small Onion, roughly chopped
4 cloves peeled garlic
1 Tbsp. fresh oregano leaves
1 pinch salt
½ tsp red pepper flakes
¼ tsp fresh ground black pepper

Process is as follows:

Place all ingredients in food processor. Process until chopped but not completely smooth. Pour into bowl, cover, and refrigerate.

Combine Marinade Ingredients
Pour Over Steak, cover and refrigerate, 12-24 hours, turning once
Cook until desired doneness. Let rest 10 minutes.
Carve Across Grain in thin slices. The thinner the better.
Serve with Chimichurri Sauce.

SHOWSTOPPER BURGERS

Juicy and flavorful extra large burgers that are a guaranteed crowd pleaser.

For 4 burgers:

2 pounds fresh ground beef (80% lean, 20% fat)
1 tablespoon Worcestershire sauce
1 1/2 teaspoons seasoning salt
1 teaspoon garlic powder
1/2 teaspoon fresh ground pepper
Optional: 4 slices of cheese
4 large hamburger buns
Choice of toppings - lettuce tomato, onion, pickles, ketchup, mustard, mayo, etc.

Process is as follows:

Preheat the grill to 375 degrees F (medium-high).

In a large bowl, add the beef. Sprinkle evenly with the Worcestershire sauce, seasoning salt, garlic powder, and pepper. Hand mix the ingredients until they are just combined.
Divide the meat mixture into fourths.

Take 1/4 of the meat mixture and use your hands to press it into the shape of a hamburger patty that is about 3/4 inch thick. Make an indention in the middle of the patty to prevent bulging in the center of the hamburger as it cooks.

Repeat with the remaining meat mixture, making 4 hamburgers.

Place the burgers on the grill. Cook 4-5 minutes on the first side. Halfway through, use spatula to turn ¼ rotation to the left to add the grill marks. Flip the burgers over and cook an additional 4-5 minutes (again making grill marks halfway through), until the burgers have reached the desired doneness (usually 4 minutes on each side for medium-well burgers).

If adding cheese, lay a slice of cheese on each burger patty about 1 minute before taking the burgers off the grill, so the cheese has a chance to melt.

Toast the buns briefly on the grill if you choose.

Serve the burgers on hamburger buns with optional toppings.

BEEF & VEGGIE SKEWERS

Perfect as an appetizer or main dish.

1/2 Cup Olive Oil
1/4 Cup Red Wine Vinegar
1/4 Cup Worcestershire Sauce
½ tsp. salt
½ tsp. pepper (always fresh ground)
1 red bell pepper cut into 1" bites
1 green bell pepper cut into 1" bites
1 medium sweet onion cut into 1" bites
3 lbs sirloin tips or filet mignon tail cut into tips (1 to 2 inches)

Process is as follows:

Mix all ingredients in zip lock bag. Refrigerate 2-4 hours. Alternate beef and vegetables on skewers (flat metal ones preferably). Discard marinade. Let loaded skewers sit in a pan at room temp for 15 minutes.

Grill on high heat for 10 minutes turning several times.

Let cool before serving.

Culinary Magic Trick

TEXAS TWINKIES (book cover bottom right photo)

Better make extra. These are a real crowd pleaser. Pair with a platter of grilled bacon wrapped shrimp for the ultimate surf and turf appetizer.

12 medium jalapeno peppers
12 Tbsp. cream cheese, softened
1 ½ pounds smoked chopped beef brisket
12 slices thick-cut bacon
½ tsp salt
½ tsp fresh ground pepper
8 oz. barbecue sauce

Process is as follows:

Preheat oven to 300 degrees

Slice jalapenos in the shape of a "T", cutting a straight vertical line from top to bottom with a cross-cut directly under the stem. Use a spoon to remove and discard all seeds and membranes.

Place on baking sheet. Bake at 300 degrees for 10 minutes.

Remove and place jalapenos in a bowl of ice water to extract the rest of the seed's oil. (*or skip this step if you like extremely spicy food)

Raise oven temp to 350 degrees. Remove jalapenos from the water and blot dry with paper towels. Spread 1 Tbsp cream cheese inside each jalapeno, then top with approx. 2 oz. of chopped smoked brisket inside each. Wrap with a slice of bacon.

Sprinkle salt and pepper over top of each and transfer to baking sheet. Cover loosely with foil to prevent bacon spatter in oven.

Bake at 350 for 30 minutes. Remove from oven and brush with the barbecue sauce. Bake for 5 minutes more.

Allow to cool before serving.

7 GRILLED CHICKEN

Techniques	72
Chart Topper Chicken	73
Key West Chicken	75
Fruit Skewer Chicken	76
Spicy Lemon Chicken	77
Smilin Time Chicken	78
Big Island Hawaiian Chicken	79
County Fair BBQ Chicken	80
Johnny Appleseed Chicken *with Veggies*	81
Teriyaki Chicken (Marinade)	82
Garlic Herb Chicken (Marinade)	83
Lemon Rosemary Chicken (Marinade)	83
Fajita Chicken (Marinade)	83
Honey Mustard Chicken (Marinade)	83

Techniques

Pound boneless, skinless chicken breasts first, between two pieces of plastic wrap. The uneven shape of boneless, skinless chicken breasts makes them tricky to grill, but by pounding the thicker end thinner, you'll reduce cooking time and have with more evenly cooked meat.

For boneless chicken breast, **turn** ¼ counter clockwise halfway through cooking on each side to make the diamond grill marks.

When cooking whole chickens, add flavor by cutting an **orange** in half and putting it in the carcass prior to grilling or smoking.

For faster grilling, **butterfly** whole chickens by cutting out the backbone so the chicken now lies flat.

Bone-In chicken is best grilled **low and slow**.

Whole chickens or chicken parts can be **injected** with marinade or sauce to add flavor. Chicken thighs work very well for this.

Add flavor before you grill by seasoning with Rusty's All Purpose Rub.

Add sauce to the exterior at the very **end** of the cooking - not before.

CHART TOPPER CHICKEN

As the name infers, this is another crowd pleaser. You can use bone-in chicken or boneless breasts, or even a combination of both. The marinade includes extra virgin olive oil, freshly squeezed lemon juice, balsamic vinegar, soy sauce, brown sugar, Worcestershire sauce, garlic, salt, and pepper.

The extra virgin olive oil keeps the chicken extra moist and juicy. The fresh lemon juice and balsamic vinegar break down the fibers in the chicken to make it tender. The soy sauce and Worcestershire sauce give it a salty depth of flavor. The brown sugar adds some rich sweetness and gives the chicken a nice crust when grilled. All of the ingredients work together in harmony to make the perfect chicken marinade.

Use whatever types of chicken you prefer — chicken breasts, thinly sliced chicken breasts, chicken tenders, or chicken thighs and legs. Chicken tenders and thinly sliced chicken breast will cook much quicker than whole pieces so watch carefully.

3 lbs. Chicken Breasts, Tenders, or Thighs and Legs
1/3 - 1/2 cup Extra Virgin Olive Oil depending on preference
3 Tablespoons Fresh Lemon Juice
3 Tablespoons Soy Sauce
2 Tablespoons Balsamic Vinegar
1/4 cup Brown Sugar
1 Tablespoon Worcestershire Sauce
3 Garlic Cloves minced or 1/2 teaspoon Garlic Powder

1 1/2 teaspoon Salt
1 teaspoon fresh ground pepper

Process is as follows:

In a bowl, stir together oil, lemon juice, soy sauce, balsamic vinegar, brown sugar, Worcestershire sauce, garlic, salt, and pepper.

Pierce chicken with a fork all over. Place in a large Ziploc bag. Pour marinade over chicken. Let marinate for at least 30 minutes. 4 - 5 hours is ideal.

Preheat grill to medium heat. Brush grill with oil to help prevent sticking.

Place chicken on the grill. Cook for approximately 6-10 minutes per side, depending on the thickness of chicken. The internal temperature of the chicken should reach 165 degrees.

Remove chicken from grill and let rest for 5 minutes.

KEY WEST CHICKEN

The Lime and Dijon Mustard combination make for an exceptional flavored dish.

1/2 cup Dijon mustard
1/4 cup lime juice
1/4 cup soy sauce
2 tablespoons minced fresh parsley or 2 teaspoons dried parsley flakes
2 tablespoons minced fresh rosemary or 2 teaspoons dried rosemary, crushed
2 tablespoons minced fresh sage or 2 teaspoons rubbed sage
2 tablespoons minced fresh thyme or 2 teaspoons dried thyme
1 teaspoon white pepper
1 teaspoon ground nutmeg
12 boneless chicken breasts (around 6 lbs)
4 medium limes, cut into wedges

Process is as follows:

Combine marinade ingredients in a small bowl. Add to chicken in large zip lock bag(s). Refrigerate for at least 4 hours.

Drain chicken, discarding marinade. Heat grill to medium.

Place chicken on the grill. Cook for approximately 5 - 6 minutes per side, depending on the thickness of chicken. The internal temperature of the chicken should reach 165 degrees.

Remove chicken from grill and let rest for 5 minutes.

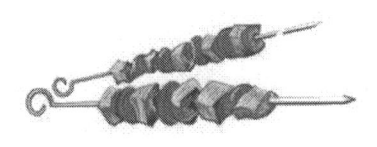

FRUIT SKEWER CHICKEN

Great as an appetizer or main dish, this is another crowd pleaser.

2 cloves garlic, finely chopped
1 tsp grated fresh ginger
4 Tbs light soy sauce
1 tsp cornstarch
2 Tbs corn syrup
4 tsp rice wine vinegar
1 tsp sugar
Kabobs (6):
1 1/2 lb boneless, skinless chicken breast – cut into 1" chunks
1 ½ cups peeled pineapple – cut into 1" chunks
1 small zucchini, peeled, – cut into 1" chunks
2 red bell peppers – cut into 1" squares
1 green bell pepper – cut into 1" squares

Process is as follows:

Combine marinade ingredients in small bowl and mix until smooth. Skewer chicken, pineapple, zucchini, red bell pepper, and green bell pepper, alternating pieces.

Brush kabobs with marinade tice on each side.
Cover and refrigerate 30-60 minues.
Grill over medium high heat 4 minutes per side, for a total of 8 minutes, or until desired doneness.

Let cool before serving.

SPICY LEMON CHICKEN

Using fresh lemons is the simple foundation of this dish. You can use bone-in chicken legs/thighs, or boneless chicken breasts if you prefer.

1/4 cup lemon juice
4 tablespoons olive oil, divided
3 tablespoons white wine
1-1/2 teaspoons crushed red pepper flakes
1 teaspoon minced fresh rosemary or 1/4 teaspoon dried rosemary, crushed
2 pounds chicken (bone-in or boneless)
2 medium lemons, halved
1 tablespoon minced chives

Process is as follows:

Combine marinade ingredients in a small bowl. Add to chicken in large zip lock bag(s). Refrigerate for at least 2 hours. Drain chicken, discarding marinade. Heat grill to medium.

Place chicken on the grill. Cook for approximately 5 - 6 minutes per side, depending on the thickness of chicken. The internal temperature of the chicken should reach 165 degrees.

Remove chicken from grill and let rest for 5 minutes.

Meanwhile, place lemons on grill, cut side down. Grill until lightly browned, 8-10 minutes. Squeeze lemon halves over chicken. Sprinkle with chives.

SMILIN TIME CHICKEN

A tangy tropical main dish guaranteed to please.

1/2 cup reduced-sodium soy sauce
1/3 cup canola oil
1/4 cup water
2 tablespoons dried minced onion
2 tablespoons sesame seeds
1 tablespoon sugar
4 garlic cloves, minced
1 teaspoon ground ginger
3/4 teaspoon salt
1/8 teaspoon cayenne pepper
5 pounds boneless chicken breasts

Process is as follows:

Combine marinade ingredients in a small bowl. Add to chicken in large zip lock bag(s). Refrigerate for at least 4 hours.

Drain chicken, discarding marinade. Heat grill to medium.

Place chicken on the grill. Cook for approximately 5 - 6 minutes per side, depending on the thickness of chicken. The internal temperature of the chicken should reach 165 degrees.

Remove chicken from grill and let rest for 5 minutes.

BIG ISLAND HAWAIIAN CHICKEN

Using boneless chicken thighs is the way to go with this one to keep it juicy.

1 cup packed brown sugar
3/4 cup ketchup
3/4 cup reduced-sodium soy sauce
1/3 cup sherry or chicken broth
2-1/2 teaspoons minced fresh gingerroot
1-1/2 teaspoons minced garlic
24 boneless skinless chicken thighs (about 6 pounds)

Process is as follows:

In a small bowl, mix the first 6 ingredients. Reserve 1-1/3 cups for basting; cover and refrigerate. Divide remaining marinade between 2 large shallow dishes.

Add 12 chicken thighs to each; turn to coat. Refrigerate, covered, for 8 hours or overnight. Drain chicken, discarding marinade.

Grill chicken, covered, on an oiled rack over medium heat for 6-8 minutes on each side or until a thermometer reads 170°; baste occasionally with reserved marinade during the last 5 minutes.

Let cool before serving.

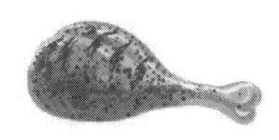

COUNTY FAIR BBQ CHICKEN

A culinary masterpiece. You can use bone-in chicken legs/thighs, or boneless chicken breasts if you prefer.

1 large onion, chopped
2/3 cup butter, melted
1/3 cup cider vinegar
4 teaspoons sugar
1 tablespoon chili powder
2 teaspoons salt
2 teaspoons Worcestershire sauce
1-1/2 teaspoons fresh ground pepper
1-1/2 teaspoons ground mustard
2 garlic cloves, minced
1/2 teaspoon hot pepper sauce
5 pounds chicken (bone-in or boneless)

Process is as follows:

Combine marinade ingredients in a small bowl. Add to chicken in large zip lock bag(s). Refrigerate for 2-4 hours. Drain chicken, discarding marinade. Heat grill to medium.

Place chicken on the grill. Cook for approximately 5 - 6 minutes per side, depending on the thickness of chicken. The internal temperature of the chicken should reach 165 degrees.

Remove chicken from grill and let rest for 5 minutes.

JOHNNY APPLESEED CHICKEN

Apple & brown sugar flavored chicken paired with vegetables.

1 cup apple juice
1/2 cup canola oil
1/4 cup packed brown sugar
1/4 cup reduced-sodium soy sauce
3 tablespoons lemon juice
2 tablespoons minced fresh parsley
3 garlic cloves, minced
8 boneless skinless chicken breast halves (6 ounces each)
4 large carrots
2 medium zucchini
2 medium yellow summer squash

Process is as follows:

In a small bowl, whisk the first seven ingredients until blended. Place 1 cup marinade and chicken in a large ziplock bag.

Refrigerate 8 hours or overnight. Cover and refrigerate remaining marinade.

Cut carrots, zucchini and squash lengthwise into quarters; cut crosswise into 2-in. pieces. Toss with 1/2 cup reserved marinade.

Drain chicken, discarding marinade in bag. Grill chicken, covered, over medium heat heat 6-8 minutes on each side or until a thermometer reads 165°, basting frequently with remaining marinade during the last 5 minutes. Keep warm.

Transfer vegetables to a grill basket and place on grill rack. Grill, covered, over medium heat 10-12 minutes or until crisp-tender, stirring frequently. Serve with chicken.

MORE SIMPLE MARINADES FOR CHICKEN

(Use Boneless Breast or Bone-In Thigh/Leg or Whole Chicken)

Be Sure To Use A Zip Lock Baggie When Marinating.

Remove Chicken from Marinade and let sit on a plate or platter for 15 minutes at room temperature before grilling.

TERIYAKI CHICKEN MARINADE
1 tbsp sesame oil
1/4 cup soy sauce
4 cloves garlic, minced
1 tbsp minced gingerroot

GARLIC HERB CHICKEN MARINADE
1/4 cup olive oil
1/4 cup dry white wine or lemon juice
4 cloves garlic, minced
1 tbsp Italian seasoning
1/2 tsp each salt & fresh ground pepper

LEMON ROSEMARY CHICKEN MARINADE
1/4 cup olive oil
1/4 cup lemon juice
1 tbsp fresh or dried rosemary
2 cloves garlic, minced
1/2 tsp each salt & fresh ground pepper

FAJITA CHICKEN MARINADE
1/4 cup olive oil
1/4 cup lime juice
1 tbs fajita seasoning (store bought)
2 1/2 tsp each salt & fresh ground pepper
**Use boneless breasts and slice thin after grilling.

HONEY MUSTARD CHICKEN MARINADE
½ cup prepared mustard
½ cup honey

EASY STREET CHICKEN
1 cup Italian Dressing (store bought)

Always discard marinade after use

Tastes Like More

8 GRILLED VEGETABLES

Tips on Grilling Vegetables	86
Grilled Corn on the Cob with husk	90
Grilled Corn on the Cob without husk	91
Grilled Bacon Wrapped Corn	92
Chart Topper Grilled Veggies	93
Lemony Grilled Zucchini	94
Grilled Fajita Veggies	96
Grilled Asparagus	98
Grilled Portobello Mushroom Burger	99
Grilled Vegetable Sandwich *with Herbed Ricotta*	100

The Best Easy Grilled Vegetables

Grilling gives a roasted smoky flavored char to what might otherwise be a dish lacking flavor. Vegetables take relatively little time to cook and are a perfect side item for any meat or seafood dish.

And much like roasted vegetables, grilling caramelizes the vegetable's sweetness by bringing out their natural sugars.

Zucchini - green or yellow work perfectly, cut into 1/3" to 1/2" slices before grilling - cut too thin and they'll fall apart.

Bell peppers, poblano peppers, jalapeño peppers, sweet baby peppers, shishito peppers - slice bell peppers and remove seeds of the bell peppers before grilling for easiest eating.

Portabello mushrooms or large brown mushrooms - no need to slice the mushrooms, grill them whole. Start the mushrooms gill side down then finish cap side down to hold in moisture.

Eggplant - grilled makes it become tender, creamy, and smoky.

Carrots - grilling quickly softens carrots and makes a pretty tiger-striped presentation.

Onions - any variety (including green) become nice and sweet when grilled.

Asparagus - fatter asparagus cooks more evenly than skinny and won't fall through the grates.

Corn - doesn't get easier than this. See tutorial on page 90.

Artichokes – outstanding flavor.

Cauliflower - slice as steaks so they hold together.

Broccoli - slice as steaks or grill in florets.

Tomatoes - best grilled only if halved. Grilled whole, they may explode and/or leak.

Helpful Tips

A **grill basket** can keep food from falling through the grates.

Slice the vegetables the **same thickness** so they cook at the same rate. Aim for slices that fall somewhere between 1/3" and 1/2". A mandolin can help in this endeavor. Note: Slicing the veggies too thin will make them too tender and may disintegrate on the grill.

Oil the veggies. Follow the golden rule of grilling when possible: oil what you grill, not the grill itself. Drizzle the vegetables with olive oil then spread it evenly with your fingers or a brush.

Season simply. Sprinkle the vegetables somewhat generously with kosher salt and freshly ground black pepper. They will absorb the salt as they cook, enhancing their inherent sweetness. Feel free to add dried herbs such as oregano, mint, tarragon, or basil if you'd like.

Grill them up **hot**. Start your veggies over medium heat, about 350°F to 450°F. Lay long slices and asparagus or carrots crosswise over the grates so they don't fall through. Close the grill lid and cook the vegetables undisturbed, flipping after 3-5 minutes.

Close the lid. Closing the lid of your grill creates the same environment as an oven, baking the vegetables as they lightly char. Check their progress minimally.

Cooking Times

Cooking times for grilled vegetables will vary depending on the thickness of your slices. Grill with the lid down to create an oven environment and check the progress of your cooking half-way through cook times.

Artichokes: Boil for 10-12 minutes then quarter and cook 4-6 minutes.

Asparagus: 6-8 minutes.

Bell pepper: Whole for 10-12 minutes; halved for 8-10 minutes.

Carrots: Boil for 4-6 minutes, then grill 3-5 minutes.

Corn: 15-20 minutes in husk. See recipes for details.

Eggplant: 5-7 minutes (thicker slices will take longer).

Portabello mushroom: 8-10 minutes.

Onion: sliced 8-10 minutes; halved 35-40 minutes.

Green onion: 3-4 minutes.

Tomato: 6-8 minutes halved.

Zucchini: 5-7 minutes.

*The veggies may look a little dry as they come off the heat, but will begin to sweat and deflate as they rest.

Serving Suggestions

Because they are just as delicious served warm or at room temperature, consider adding a simple topping or sauce, like:

Sprinkle veggies with shredded parmesan cheese or crumbled feta or goat cheese.

Drizzle with garlicky chimichurri sauce, creamy avocado salsa verde, or balsamic glaze.

Add a dollop of goat cheese, homemade basil pesto or arugula pesto.

GRILLED CORN ON THE COB

Great with olive oil or butter, salt, and pepper. For a spicy twist, rub with ccilantro lime butter then sprinkle with chopped cilantro and red pepper flakes.

Cilantro Lime Butter: In a small bowl, mix 2 tablespoons finely chopped cilantro with ¼ teaspoon lime zest, and 1/2 teaspoon sea salt. Mash in 1/4 cup softened unsalted butter until well combined. Roll into a log, wrap in parchment paper, and chill until firm.

Here are two methods for how to grill corn on the cob. Each provides a slightly different result, but both are delicious. Choose the first one if you like your corn sweeter and juicier, and choose the second if you want it to have a smoky, charred flavor from the grill.

Method 1: In the husk (very little char) – In this method, the ears of corn steam inside the husk, yielding juicy, tender kernels that are bright yellow and barely charred. Pull the husks of the corn back, leaving them attached at the base, and remove the silk (as much as you can). Next, pull the husks back up and soak the corn in the husks for 10 minutes in a pot of cold water (Soaking corn hydrates the husks, preventing them from burning too much on the grill). Remove, drain, and pat dry with paper towels. Then grill it in the husks until the corn is tender and light char marks form. Heat a grill to medium-high heat. Place the corn on the grill and cook, turning every 3 to 5 minutes, until all sides of the corn are cooked, about 15 minutes. Remove from the grill, tie back the husks and use them as a handle. Serve with desired toppings.

Method 2: Straight on the grill (provides char) – Shuck the corn, removing the silk and husks, and cook the cobs directly on the grill. Cooking corn this way means that the kernels won't be quite as juicy – they'll lose some of their moisture to the hot grill grates. However, they'll be nicely charred and full of smoky flavor. This method is also great if you're short on time. With no soaking required, the grilled corn cooks up in minutes.

4 to 8 ears fresh corn

Topping options:

    Butter, sea salt, lemon or lime wedges, red pepper flakes

    Cilantro Lime Butter

    Ranch Dressing

GRILLED BACON WRAPPED CORN

This tasty dish is easy to prepare and works great as an appetizer or side dish.

8 Ears sweet yellow corn.
About 1 ½ pounds thick sliced bacon (16 slices)

Process is as follows:

Husk and wash ears of yellow corn.
Wrap in bacon at an angle, usually 2 slices covers the corn.
Wrap individual ears in heavy duty aluminum foil.
Preheat grill to hot.

Grill corn 10 minutes per side (Turning 3 times over 30 minutes)

Turn heat to low or grill over indirect heat 45 minutes until bacon is cooked and corn tender.

Let cool before serving.

CHART TOPPER GRILLED VEGGIES

Great as a side dish with beef, chicken, or seafood.

Zucchini, bell pepper, onions, asparagus, and mushrooms become sweet and savory when cooked on the grill. With just a brushing of olive oil and sprinkling of salt and pepper, this cooking method is simple and lets the vegetables natural goodness shine through.

2 portabello mushrooms
1 eggplant
1 zucchini
1 yellow squash
1 onion
1 bunch thick asparagus
1 red bell pepper
2 tablespoons extra virgin olive oil
1 tablespoon kosher salt
1 tablespoon fresh ground black pepper

Process is as follows:

Prepare the grill with clean grates and preheat to medium heat, 350°F to 450°F.

Trim the ends of the eggplant, zucchini, yellow squash and onion and cut into 1/3" to 1/2" slices. Seed the red bell pepper and cut into quarters. Trim the ends of the asparagus.

Drizzle the vegetables with olive oil and sprinkle evenly with salt and pepper. Grill the vegetables with the lid closed until tender and lightly charred all over, about 8 to 10 minutes for the bell peppers, onion, and mushroom; 5-7 minutes for the yellow squash, zucchini, and eggplant and asparagus.

Serve warm or at room temperature.

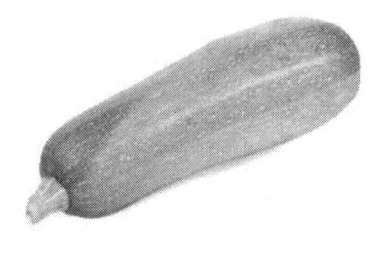

LEMONY GRILLED ZUCCHINI

Simple grilled zucchini wedges are delicious on their own, but a lemony yogurt sauce, feta, and mint really elevate them in this easy recipe.

3 small-medium zucchini, quartered lengthwise, cut in half horizontally
Extra-virgin olive oil, for drizzling
Sea salt and fresh ground black pepper
Juice of 1 small lemon

lemony yogurt, with feta & mint:
½ cup whole milk Greek yogurt
Zest of 1 small lemon
½ garlic clove, finely minced
¼ cup crumbled feta cheese
¼ cup fresh mint
Pinch of red pepper flakes
1 tsp. each Sea salt and fresh ground pepper

Process is as follows:

Preheat a grill to high heat. Toss the zucchini lightly with olive oil and pinches of salt and pepper. Grill cut side-down for 2 minutes, then flip and grill skin-side down for 3 to 4 minutes or until char marks form.

Remove from the grill, transfer to a plate, and squeeze with lemon juice.

In a small bowl, mix together the yogurt, lemon zest, garlic, and ¼ teaspoon salt. Spread the yogurt on a medium serving platter, top with the zucchini, feta, mint, and red pepper flakes.

Season to taste and serve.

GRILLED FAJITA VEGGIES

Great on a burrito, a salad, or just a side item. Slice them thin to win.

3 multi-colored peppers, stemmed and sliced into strips
3 portobello mushrooms, stemmed and wiped clean
1 red onion, sliced into wedges
2 tablespoons avocado oil
2 garlic cloves, chopped
½ teaspoon chili powder, more to taste
½ teaspoon cumin
½ teaspoon sea salt, more to taste
Splash of balsamic vinegar
2 limes, sliced into wedges
½ teaspoon fresh ground pepper

Serving Suggestions:

>Flour or Corn Tortillas
>Choice of Protein (Chicken, Steak, Shrimp)
>Guacamole or avocado slices squeezed with lime
>Tomatillo Salsa or Pineapple Salsa
>Diced tomatoes or Pico de Gallo
>Pickled Jalapeños or sliced plain jalapeños
>Cilantro

Process is as follows:

Heat a grill to medium heat with a 12-inch cast-iron skillet (or grill pan) inside.

Arrange the peppers on a tray and the mushrooms and onion wedges on a separate rimmed plate. In a small bowl, whisk together the avocado oil, garlic, chili powder, cumin, salt, and several grinds of pepper. Drizzle 1 scant tablespoon of the mixture over the peppers and toss to coat. Drizzle the remaining marinade over the mushrooms and onions. Drizzle the mushrooms with a splash of balsamic vinegar and use your hands to coat the mushrooms on both sides.

Grill the peppers in the cast-iron pan for 8 to 10 minutes, tossing occasionally, until charred and soft. Be careful not to overfill the pan or the veggies won't char on the edges - cook them in 2 batches, if necessary. Grill the mushrooms and onion wedges directly on the grill for about 4 minutes about per side. Remove everything from the grill, using a potholder to remove the cast-iron pan. Squeeze the juice of ½ lime over the peppers and season with salt, pepper, and more chili powder, to taste. Slice the mushrooms into strips and place on a serving dish. Transfer the onions and the peppers to a serving skillet or large platter.

Serve with the tortillas, guacamole, jalapeños, tomatoes, cilantro, salsa, and remaining lime wedges for serving.

GRILLED ASPARAGUS

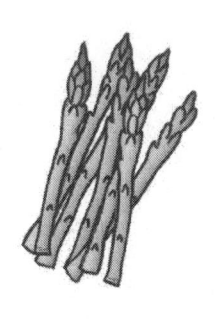

This grilled asparagus recipe goes well with just about anything. Serve it simple style - with salt, pepper, and a squeeze of lemon juice

First, trim the bottom of the asparagus spears to remove the woody ends. You can trim the spears with a knife, or use your hands to break them. Hold the end of a spear in one hand, and bend the spear until it snaps. It should break in just the right spot — where the woody part ends and the tender part begins.

Next toss the trimmed asparagus with olive oil, salt, and pepper.

Preheat a grill to medium-high heat, and grill the spears for 6 to 8 minutes, flipping halfway through. Using a grill basket is helpful to not have them fall through the cooking grates. The asparagus is ready when it's fork-tender and lightly charred. Remove it from the heat, and enjoy!

For an extra boost of flavor, grill lemon halves alongside the asparagus. Drizzle the cut sides with olive oil, season them with salt and pepper, and grill the halves cut-side-down until grill marks form. When you're ready to eat, squeeze the charred lemon juice over the asparagus spears.

GRILED PORTOBELLO BURGER

This mushroom burger has a tangy and savory charred flavor. Be sure to toast the bun before loading it up.

Remove the stems from the mushrooms and use a damp towel to wipe the caps clean.

Drizzle them generously with olive oil, balsamic & tamari and sprinkle them with salt & fresh ground pepper. Use your hands to make sure they're fully coated — it'll be a little messy, but the better coated your burgers are, the more flavorful they will be!

Preheat your grill to medium and put on the mushrooms, starting with the gill side up. Grill for 4-5 minutes per side, until the mushrooms are tender and grill marks form.

Top with your favorite fixings, and enjoy!

Serving Suggestions

The grilled portobellos are just as good with classic fixings like ketchup, mustard, mayo, pickles, and onion. You may want to try a scoop of guacamole, a slather of tzatziki and/or a dollop of chipotle sauce.

GRILLED VEGETABLE SANDWICH WITH HERBED RICOTTA

The combination of flavors is really unique with this one. Delicious is an understatement. Use fresh herbs if you can.

You can make your own balsamic glaze by bringing 1/2 cup of balsamic vinegar and 2 tablespoons of sugar to a boil in a small saucepan, then reduce to a simmer and cook until reduced by half, for about 20 minutes. Store bought is fine too.

1 cup ricotta cheese
1 tablespoon each of fresh basil chives and parsley, chopped
1 clove garlic minced
1 tablespoon extra virgin olive oil plus more for drizzling
½ teaspoon each: kosher salt & fresh ground pepper
1 portobello mushroom
1 medium zucchini sliced lengthwise
1 medium yellow squash sliced lengthwise
1/2 medium eggplant sliced into rounds
1/2 red onion peeled and sliced into rounds
1/2 red bell pepper seeded and sliced in half or quarters
2 teaspoons dried oregano
1 loaf ciabatta bread or other soft bread sliced into 6-inch sections and cut in half
1/2 cup arugula leaves
Balsamic glaze

Process is as follows:

In a small bowl, combine the ricotta cheese, fresh herbs, garlic clove, 1 tablespoon extra virgin olive oil, kosher salt and freshly ground black pepper and mix until smooth. Set aside.

Oil the grill grates with paper towels lightly coated with grapeseed or canola oil. Preheat the grill on medium high for 10-15 minutes.

Drizzle the vegetables with extra virgin olive oil and season with dried oregano and kosher salt and pepper.

Drizzle some additional olive oil on the cut side of the ciabatta.

Place the vegetables on the grill and cook undisturbed for 5 minutes. Gently flip veggies with a spatula when veggies start to soften and grill marks develop. Cook for another 5 minutes. Toast the cut sides of the ciabatta. Transfer the veggies and ciabatta to a platter.

Spread the herbed ricotta mixture on the cut sides of the bread slices. Top the bottom bread slices with layers of grilled vegetables and arugula then drizzle with balsamic glaze.

Serve warm or at room temperature.

Tastes Like More

GRILLED GINGER HONEY SALMON

This is a delicious dish that's healthy in Omega's and other vitamins to boost your energy.

Ginger Honey Marinade

1/3 cup orange juice
1/3 cup reduced-sodium soy sauce
1/4 cup honey
1 green onion, chopped
1 teaspoon ground ginger
1 teaspoon garlic powder

1 salmon fillet (1 1/2 pounds and 3/4 inch thick)

Process is as follows:

For marinade, mix first six ingredients. In a shallow bowl, combine salmon and 2/3 cup marinade; refrigerate 30 minutes, turning occasionally. Reserve remaining marinade for basting.

Place salmon on an oiled grill rack over medium heat, skin side down; discard marinade remaining in bowl. Grill salmon, covered, until fish just begins to flake easily with a fork, 15-18 minutes, basting with reserved marinade during the last 5 minutes.

Let cool before serving.

with the sauce in the larger bowl, toss with shrimp and vegetables. Let stand 15 minutes.

Alternately thread shrimp and vegetables onto 8 metal (preferably flat) skewers.

Grill, covered, over medium heat until shrimp turn pink, 3-4 minutes per side.

Serve on bed of additional herbs with crusty bread and reserved sauce.

BACON-WRAPPED GRILLED SHRIMP

This is the ultimate appetizer. For an interesting twist, add these to a toasted hoagie roll with shredded iceberg lettuce, thin sliced tomatoes, and a little mayo for a shrimp po' boy sandwich that is out of this world.

½ Tspn Cayenne Pepper
½ Tspn Cumin
½ Tspn Citrus Lemon Pepper
1/4 Tspn Garlic Powder
1 TBspn Worcestershire sauce
1 TBspn Fresh Squeezed Lemon Juice
4 TBspn Butter, melted
10 Slices Bacon
20 Large Shrimp - Peeled and deveined

Process is as follows:

Use flat metal skewers which make turning the shrimp on the grill easier.

Combine butter and spices, add shrimp and stir to coat.

Cover and marinate in refrigerator for 30 minutes.

Slice bacon in half and cook in skillet to halfway done, keeping bacon flexible. Drain bacon and pat dry on paper towel.

Wrap each shrimp with piece of bacon and slide onto skewer.

Grill on high heat for approximately 3 minutes on each side (until shrimp are opaque and bacon is done and crispy).

Let cool before serving.

CAJUN GRILLED FISH FILETS

Healthy, tasty, and loaded with flavor. Pair with a steak for a delicious surf and turf combo.

3/4 cup canola oil
1 medium onion, finely chopped
2 tablespoons Cajun seasoning
6 garlic cloves, minced
2 teaspoons ground cumin
1 teaspoon minced fresh rosemary
1 teaspoon minced fresh thyme

4 fish filets - preferably arund 1 ½ inches thick
Tuna, Swordfish, Snapper, Mahi Mahi, Sea Bass, or equivalent

Process is as follows:

Mix ingredients in a glass dish (do not use metal). Add fish to the marinade and turn to coat. Cover and refrigerate 1 hour.

Lightly oil grill grate and grill on high heat for 3 minutes, then turn ¼ counter clockwise to add diamond grill marks and cook an additional 3 minutes.

Flip and repeat process. Cut into one of the filets to test doneness, as it should be cooked all the way through.

Serve on a platter with lemon wedges.

GRILLED LEMON GARLIC SEA SCALLOPS

Crispy outside, tender and juicy inside. Great as an appetizer or main dish.

1/4 cup olive oil
juice of one lemon
3 garlic cloves minced
1 Tbsp Italian seasoning
½ tsp salt and ½ tsp fresh ground pepper

1 1/2 pounds large sea scallops

Process is as follows:

In a medium sized glass bowl combine olive oil, lemon juice, garlic, and Italian seasoning.

Salt and pepper the scallops and add to the bowl and toss in marinade to coat. Cover and marinate in the fridge for about 30 minutes.

Place the scallops on a grill over medium high heat for 2-3 minutes on each side or until cooked throughout and slightly charred.

Serve on a platter with lemon wedges.

KEY WEST GRILLED TUNA STEAKS

¼ cup orange juice
¼ cup soy sauce
¼ cup olive oil
2 Tbsp fresh squeezed lemon juice
2 Tbps chopped fresh parsley
1 clove garlic, minced

½ tspn chopped fresh oregano
½ tspn fresh ground pepper
4 tuna steaks, preferably about 1 ½ inches thick (about six ounces each)

Process is as follows:

In a large glass dish, mix together the orange juice, soy sauce, olive oil, lemon juice, parsley, garlic, oregano, and pepper.

Place the tuna steaks in the marinade and turn to coat. Cover, and refrigerate for one hour.

Lightly oil grill grate and grill on high heat for 3 minutes, then turn ¼ counter clockwise to add diamond grill marks and cook an additional 3 minutes.

Flip and repeat process. Cut into one of the tuna steaks to test doneness, as it should be cooked all the way through.

Serve on a platter with lemon wedges.

Tastes Like More

DOCTOR: Do you smoke?

PATIENT: Yeah.

DOCTOR: Cigarettes? Marijuana?

PATIENT: Mostly Brisket and Pork.

10 NOW FOR SMOKING

Easy Does It	116
Times	117
Wood Chips	118
Boston Butt (pork shoulder)	118
Baby Back Ribs	119
Cherry Candy Beef Brisket	120
Honey Glazed Whole Chickens	121
Mello Yellow Boston Butt	122
Apple Wood Smoked Salmon	123
Butter Infused Smoked Turkey	124
Standing Rib Roast	125
Teriyaki Chicken Wings	126
Chicken and Sausage Kabobs	127

EASY DOES IT...

If you recall, at the outset of the book we took a look at different varieties of smokers, all of which can produce great barbecue. But the title of this book includes the word "easy"... and that is why I am suggesting you invest in an **Orion Cooker**.

The makers of the Orion describe it as follows:

The Orion Cooker
Load Light Eat

"As an all-in-one convection cooker and meat smoker, the Orion Cooker is the outdoor charcoal grill for master grillers, occasional cooks, and all who love succulent, flavorful meat without a long wait or major effort!"

Culinary Magic Trick

*Moist, tender, and tasty meat in a fraction of the time and effort.

Orion General Cooking Times (times are approximate)

Beef Brisket	6-7 pounds	3 hours
	13-14 pounds	4 hours 30 min
Baby Back Ribs	3-6 racks (slabs)	1 hour 15 minutes
Boston Butt	5 pounds	4 hours
	Two 5-7 pounds	5 hours
Salmon Filet	2-3 pounds	30 minutes
Chicken Wings	40 wings	1 hour
Pork Chops	1 ½ in. thick	40 minutes
Turkey (Whole)	15 pounds	1 hr 45 min
	20 pounds	2 hr 15 min
Prime Rib	7 pounds	1 hr 30 min
Whole Chicken	3-4 pounds	1 hour 10 min

Wood chip recommendations:

ALDER WOOD chips	Salmon
APPLE WOOD chips	Pork, Poultry, Sausage
APRICOT WOOD chips	Fish, Shrimp, Chicken
CHERRY WOOD chips	Pork, Chicken, Turkey
HICKORY WOOD chips	Brisket, Ribs, Pork, Chicken,
By far the most popular	Turkey
MESQUITE WOOD chips	Pork, Fish
PEACH WOOD chips	Pork, Chicken
PECAN WOOD chips	Pork

BOSTON BUTT (for Pulled, Chopped, or Sliced Pork) On a bun, a plate, or a platter, this is a crowd pleaser every time. Have a variety of sauces for guests to choose.

Rub generously with Rusty's All Purpose BBQ Rub. Cover and refrigerate overnight.

Bring to room temperature. Prepare cooker. Hickory wood chips recommended. Cook at 50 minutes per pound. 5 pound butt = 4 hr. 10 min.

Remove and wrap in aluminum foil. Then wrap in a towel and put into an empty cooler for 1 hour.

Pull or chop for serving.

BABY BACK RIBS

Tender and smoked to perfection. To add an extra char, put on a high heat grill for 3-4 minutes per side after smoking.

6 racks (slabs) ribs

Rinse ribs, pat dry, and trim fat.

Coat both sides with Rusty's All Purpose BBQ Rub. Cover and leave in fridge overnight.

Affix ribs to hangers in cooker.

Use cherry or hickory wood chips.

Cook 1 hr 15 minutes. Char on grill if desired.

Cut each slab into 3 rib portions and serve on a platter.

Add sauce on side in small bowls.

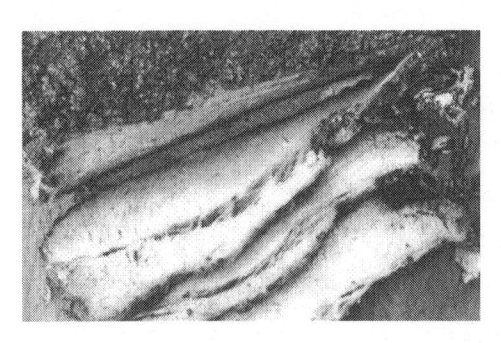

BBQ BEEF BRISKET

(Sliced or Chopped) The bark is often referred to as candy. Inject the Brisket with Cherry Coke before smoking and you'll see why.

12 pound brisket.

Cut brisket in half. Trim fat if needed.

Soak in apple cider vinegar 8 hours (covered in fridge).

Remove and pat dry with paper towels. Inject several places into top layer of each brisket with 1 can of cherry coke.

Rub with Rusty's Red Neck BBQ Rub.

Fill drip pan ½ full with equal parts apple cider vinegar and water.

Place larger cut of brisket on bottom grate and smaller one on middle grate.

6 pound brisket = 3 hr. (30 minutes per pound)

Remove and wrap in aluminum foil. Then wrap in a towel and put into an empty cooler for 1 hour.

Slice or chop for serving (I prefer chopped).

Provide different sauces to choose from.

HONEY GLAZED WHOLE CHICKENS

This recipe will provide a lot of food for not a lot of money. It's a great way to feed a crowd and please both the light and dark meat fans.

4 Chickens (3-4 pounds each)

Apply light glaze of honey on exterior.

Coat in Rusty's All Purpose BBQ Rub.

Put 2 Chickens on lower grate and 2 on middle or upper grate depending on size.

Cook 1 hr 30 minutes

Cut off wings and legs and pull the rest of the meat and chop it. Serve on a platter with the pile of chopped chicken in the center.

Have sauces on hand for those who choose to add it.

MELLO YELLOW BOSTON BUTT

A nice twist on an old favorite. As long as you are firing up the cooker, it is recommended to cook at least 2 butts.

2 to 3 5-8 pound pork butts. Trim fat. Pierce all sides of meat several times with fork.

Pour 3 liter bottle of Mello Yellow soda in large pot and add pork.

Cover and refrigerate 24 hours.

Remove from pot and pat dry with paper towels. Discard marinade.

Coat thoroughly with Rusty's All Purpose BBQ Rub.

Use ½ hickory and ½ mesquite wood chips.

Place meat fat side up on top-level grate (and mid-level grate if more room is needed for additional).

Cook 50 minutes per pound.

Remove and wrap in aluminum foil. Then wrap in a towel and put into an empty cooler for 1 hour.

Pull or chop for serving. Sauces optional.

APPLE WOOD SMOKED SALMON FILET

A delicacy from the sea that is great as a main dish and also pairs well with steak for a surf and turf combo.

2 Tablespoons brown sugar
2 teaspoons black pepper (fresh ground)
1 teaspoon coarse ground sea salt
1/2 teaspoon dried basil
1/2 teaspoon garlic powder
1/2 teaspoon smoked paprika

Combine all ingredients in a bowl, using a fork or whisk to break up any clumps. Use the seasoning immediately on the filets.

Use apple wood chips in the cooker.

From 3 lemons, cut slices 1/8 inch thick, place on top of salmon filets. Put filets on top grate.

Cook roughly 30 minutes. Filet will be cooked when meat is flaky.

BUTTER INFUSED SMOKED TURKEY

Any day can be Thanksgiving with this easy to make dish. Invite a crowd over the enjoy the feast.

12-20 pound turkey
1 stick butter, melted
Olive Oil
Rusty's All Purpose Rub

Process is as follows:

Wash and pat dry turkey. Rub exterior with olive oil. Cover with Rusty's All Purpose Rub. Inject the melted butter into serveral places on each side.

Use cherry wood chips in the cooker. Cook 7 minutes per pound. Check with thermometer at end of cooking (165 degrees internal).

Tip: Wrap turkey with 4 or 5 butcher strings to hold it together, as it becomes very delicate near end of cooking.

HICKORY SMOKED STANDING RIB ROAST
(Prime Rib)

Delicious every time. Your guests will agree.

7-8 lbs standing rib roast

Rusty's All Purpose Rub

Hickory Chips to be in the cooker.

Apply rub evenly on all sides of the roast.

Place meat on the middle cooking grate.

Check after 1.5 hours for doneness.

Let cool before slicing. Serve slices on a platter with sides of Au Jus and Horseradish Sauce.

TERIYAKI SMOKED CHICKEN WINGS

The perfect appetizer for any gathering.

40 chicken wings

Teriyaki Marinade (see page 35)

Process is as follows:

Wash wings and pat dry. Marinate for one hour.

Place wings on center and top grate of cooker.

Use Hickory wood chips.

Cook 1 hour.

Serve on a platter with Ranch or Blue Cheese Dressing.

CHICKEN AND SMOKED SAUSAGE KABOBS

Great as an appetizer or main course.

2 pounds boneless chicken breast

2 pounds smoked sausage

Process is as follows:

Wash and pat dry chicken and sausage. Cut into approx. 1 inch squares. Load onto metal skewers, alternating chicken and sausage.

Coat with Rusty's All Purpose Rub and cook 1 hour on the top and center grates.

Let cool before serving.

Tastes Like More

(*left to right:* Bud Anderson, Cal Harrison, Andy Weddle, Adam Fisher)

THE "SULTANS OF SWINE"

FIRST TROPHY

2006